Jenny Alexander grew up in London, and went to university there. She spent the next 20 years living and working in various parts of the UK, and bringing up her four children.

In recent years she has written several children's stories. The first, *Stumpy-Toe* (Hamish Hamilton, 1995), was about bullying. The second, *Miss Fischer's Jewels* (Hamish Hamilton, 1996), was about the importance of expressing emotion. Other stories have tackled themes of conquering fear and prejudice and having the courage to be yourself.

Faced with the problem of bullying in real life, she and her children looked for creative and effective ways of coping, and *Your Child: Bullying* grew naturally out of that experience.

YOUR CHILD SERIES

A series of books containing easy-to-follow, practical advice for the parents of children with a variety of illnesses or conditions.

Each book provides a clear overview of the situation, explaining essential information about the illness or condition and outlining the practical steps parents can take to help understand, support and care for their child, the rest of the family as well as themselves. Guiding parents through the conventional, the complementary and the alternative approaches which are available, these books cater for children of all ages, ranging from babies to teenagers, and enable the whole family to move forward in a positive way.

Titles in *Your Child* series:

Your Child: Asthma by Erika Harvey
Your Child: Bullying by Jenny Alexander
Your Child: Diabetes by Catherine Steven
Your Child: Eczema by Maggie Jones

YOUR CHILD

Bullying
Practical and Easy-to-Follow Advice

Jenny Alexander

ELEMENT

Shaftesbury, Dorset • Boston, Massachusetts
Melbourne, Victoria

First published in Great Britain in 1998 by
Element Books Limited
Shaftesbury, Dorset SP7 8BP

Published in the USA in 1998 by
Element Books, Inc.
160 North Washington Street
Boston, MA 02114

Published in Australia in 1998 by
Element Books and distributed
by Penguin Australia Ltd
487 Maroondah Highway, Ringwood,
Victoria 3134

Reprinted 1998

Cover design by Slatter Andersen
Design by Roger Lightfoot
Typeset by Footnote Graphics, Warminster, Wilts
Printed and bound in Great Britain by
Creative Print and Design (Wales), Ebbw Vale

British Library Cataloguing in Publication
data available

Library of Congress Cataloging in Publication data
Alexander, Jenny.
Your child : bullying : practical and easy-to-follow advice /
Jenny Alexander.
p.   cm.
Includes bibliographical references and index.
1. Bullying.   2. Child rearing.   I. Title.
BF637.B85A44   1998
649.—cc21   98–11292
                                                    CIP

ISBN 1 86204 206 3

The author and publishers are grateful for permission to reprint the following
copyright material:

Jung, C G; *Jung's Collected Works*, Volume 9 (Routledge, 1968) p. 175.
Copyright © 1959; 1969; 1972 by Princeton University Press. Reprinted by
permission of Princeton University Press and Routledge.

Children are educated by what the grown-up is, and not by what he says.

C G Jung (*Collected Works*, Vol. 9)

Contents

Acknowledgements

I should like to thank all the authors whose work on so many different subjects has contributed to my understanding of the bullying problem over the years. I am particularly grateful to Susan Jeffers for giving me permission to use her 'pushing back your boundaries' and to Penny Parks for her 'inner child rescue scene'.

Thanks also to Routledge and Princeton University Press for permission to use the quotation from C G Jung.

I am grateful to my agent, Sara Menguc, and my publisher, without whose faith and enthusiasm this book would not have been written.

I want to thank my husband, Ian, for his unfailing friendship and support.

But most of all, I thank my children, whose experience of bullying has taught me so much about my own.

Introduction

I want to say at the outset that this is not a general book on the subject of bullying – it's a self-help book for parents whose children are being bullied. It does not contain any facts and figures, statistics and psychological profiles, because its subject is the practical day-to-day challenge of helping your child to cope with bullying.

If this book had been available when my child was being bullied, I think it could have saved my family several months of acute anxiety and pain. That's why I'm writing it for you.

Bullying is a shocking problem. First, there's the shock of finding out how unutterably cruel children can be to each other. Then, for parents, there's the shock of suddenly having to deal with a child under extreme stress and, finally, there's the shock of discovering that when your child is being bullied you become a victim, too.

His unhappiness makes you unhappy; his fear makes you afraid. If he dreads going to school, you dread sending him. You feel the same impotent anger about the situation he's in; towards the people who are making him suffer, you feel the same murderous hate.

I didn't want my child to be a victim and I didn't want to be one either. So I wrote off to all the bullying organizations and ordered all the recommended books, looking for ideas about how to take effective action.

I found that the conventional advice to parents falls into two main categories – how to get your child's school to help, and how to get your child to help himself.

As soon as my husband and I opened a dialogue with the school it occurred to me that even if they managed to stop the bullying our child would still be vulnerable. Children who have been bullied are likely to be bullied again, simply because a precedent has been set. Children who are bullied repeatedly become less and less able to defend themselves. It was up to the school to sort out the current situation, but it was up to my child to learn to stay safe.

Unfortunately, most of the advice I found about what to tell a bullied child seemed to be either so obvious that he would already be doing it – like avoiding the places where the people doing the bullying hung out – or else, quite frankly, impractical. It was only because I couldn't think what else to do that I tried it, and I certainly wish I hadn't.

It might sound fine in theory to say that bullied children should tell a teacher, pretend they don't care, act more assertively, join clubs and make new friends, but, as you will probably know if your child is being bullied, these are not real options for children whose self-esteem has taken a battering. Asking fragile children to do such things is setting them up for failure, and their failure will just make you feel more frustrated and helpless than ever.

I reached the conclusion that the conventional approach – trying to get bullied children to change their behaviour without first addressing their feelings – was putting the cart before the horse. It was pointless to ask children who felt bad about themselves to pretend they didn't, but if they felt good about themselves their behaviour would automatically change anyway. So how could you make someone feel good about himself? I didn't know, but I knew how to find out.

Back to the bookshops and library I went, this time looking not for books on bullying, but for books on positive thinking, building self-esteem and coping with the high levels of anger and fear my child was feeling.

These books, which I should never have dreamed of reading before, turned out to be packed with uplifting anecdotes, memorable quotations and practical exercises. I was sure the ideas in them could help my child, but they were all adult books and I couldn't find anything similar written for children.

I decided to try the ideas out for myself. After all, I was a victim, too. I had my own unhappiness, fear and anger about the bullying situation to deal with. If my child wanted to join in, too, he could, because I would explain what I was doing as I went along.

I started with positive thinking: it looked as if it would be easy and fun. I explained it to my children in terms of positive and negative words, and to illustrate the point I suggested we try to use only positive words for a whole mealtime. It was a sort of game.

We all enjoyed it, and the children wanted to know more. Over the next few weeks the older ones got stuck into some of the less complicated books, and even the younger two, then aged eight and six, had no difficulty at all in grasping the essentials.

Positive thinking helped the whole family to feel calmer and more in control, and that meant our house became a better environment for reviving our bullied child's failing optimism and zest for life.

We went on to consider ways of creating an environment that would be particularly nurturing to self-esteem, and we looked at how to meet the challenge of coping with unusually high levels of fear and anger in more robust and positive ways.

The programme we developed worked surprisingly well. I had hoped that it would help my child feel happier and more self-confident, and that coping better with the teasing that was still going on would mean he didn't bring so much stress home into the family. I had also hoped that it would make me feel less of a victim myself.

In the event, it achieved much more. Because what I had failed to anticipate was that as soon as the bullying stopped mattering so much to my child, it would stop.

All the ideas that worked for us are brought together in this book. It's a brief and subjective selection, and if you want to explore any of the areas in greater depth I have included a further reading list at the end.

Some of the ideas may seem simple and obvious to you, and others difficult. I'm sure there will be some things you just don't agree with. Everyone's different. But I hope there will be something here that will help you to find a sense of direction and purpose, if what is happening has left you and your child feeling helpless and bewildered.

The book opens with a couple of chapters on how to establish the facts and get help if you need to, but the rest of the book is all about self-help.

I have started with the least challenging areas, because that seems to me the easiest way to work. Besides, getting rid of blame, developing a positive mental attitude and building good self-esteem are the best possible preparation for tackling the really hot topics of anger and fear.

Within each chapter I have worked in the same way, applying the ideas to non-challenging, general situations before suggesting that you try to apply them directly to the problem of bullying.

I haven't made any distinction at all between different age groups of children, because this approach is about developing the robust attitudes in yourself that you want your child to have, and so providing a strong role model for him. Whether your child is 5 or 15 he will learn by what you are, and it doesn't really matter what you say, so there's no need to tailor anything here to his particular stage of development.

I haven't distinguished either between the various sorts of people who might be doing the bullying. Although my child's experience was school-based, a lot of bullying occurs outside school and can involve adults as well as children. But, whoever is doing the bullying, the effects on the person being bullied are the same, and this approach concentrates on tackling the effects.

By the same token, I haven't gone into all the apparent reasons why your child might be being bullied. Whether your child is abused for being black or white, male or female, fat or thin, high-achieving or low-achieving, popular or solitary, makes no difference. The effects are still the same.

The whole point about bullying for people who bully is to make someone else feel bad about himself. Loss of self-confidence, low self-esteem, incapacitating anxiety and helpless rage are the effects the person who bullies is looking for. When he can no longer produce them in your child he will find a more satisfying victim.

Anyone who is being bullied needs to develop expertise in psychological self-defence to protect his self-image and handle high levels of anger and fear. The only difference for people who stand out from the crowd in any obvious way, or have long-term problems with bullying, is that they may need to use these skills more often.

The great thing about the skills your child needs to cope with bullying is that they will also help him to meet all his future challenges and setbacks with much greater courage and confidence, and enable him to realize his full potential in every area of his life.

Working together to master these skills requires perseverance and commitment but, unlike more conventional ideas, it works. Also, unlike the conventional approach, it makes full use of your child's most valuable resource – you.

Note: 'He' and 'she' have been used to describe your child in alternate chapters to avoid the more cumbersome 'he or she'.

Chapter One

Getting the Facts

The kind of facts you don't need to know, as a parent, are what proportion of boys or girls who bully have poor physical hygiene and what percentage of children under ten are very worried/a bit worried/not worried at all about being bullied.

Focusing on statistics is unhelpful because it encourages you to think of children as 'victims' and 'bullies', instead of seeing the bullying situation as only a part of their lives. It can have you wondering what is wrong with your child that has made him into a victim or a bully. This kind of approach is backward-looking and passive – it does nothing to make you feel less angry and bewildered.

If you want to move to the more active position of looking for solutions instead of explanations the only facts you need to know are:

What is bullying?

and

Is your child being bullied?

WHAT IS BULLYING?

There are two main categories of bullying – physical and non-physical.

Physical bullying includes kicking, hitting, pushing, spitting, damage to property, theft and extortion.

Non-physical bullying includes teasing, name-calling,
threatening, excluding
and whispering campaigns.

In the past, people have tended to regard physical bullying as
more serious than non-physical bullying, partly because the
activities involved in physical bullying are illegal in adult life. But
times are changing.

Psychological harm is now regarded as grounds for prosecution.
In Britain there are new anti-stalking laws, and in a recent test
case a 12-year-old girl had her claim of common assault against an
older child upheld in court, even though the aggression she
suffered was purely verbal. In another case, a boy who sued his
school for failing to protect him from racist taunts was awarded
significant damages.

We can only judge how serious bullying is by the effects it has
on the people involved, and this will depend on many factors
other than what form the bullying takes.

One thing we can say categorically is that it is a very rare case
of bullying that results in long-term physical damage, whereas all
forms of bullying can leave psychological scars that last a lifetime.

For this reason, if your child seems upset and unsettled and you
don't know why, it is certainly worthwhile trying to find out
whether he's being bullied.

IS YOUR CHILD BEING BULLIED?

Quite often, parents have no idea that their child is being bullied
until a particularly nasty incident blows the whole situation wide
open, or a teacher draws their attention to it, or the child
suddenly breaks down. But more often than not there are small
signs and symptoms of what is going on.

Some physical signs of bullying are:

• cuts and bruises, lost dinner money, damage to clothes and
  property

- minor ailments, like headaches and stomach upsets
- eating disorders
- sleeplessness and nightmares
- bedwetting

Some social signs are:

- lack of enthusiasm about having friends over or going out
- loss of interest in hobbies and pastimes
- reluctance to go to school

Some psychological effects of bullying are:

- heightened levels of anxiety and mood swings
- outbursts of rage
- destructive or self-destructive behaviour
- bouts of apathy and depression
- over-sensitivity to criticism

There may also be a reduction of effort and competence in school work.

The problem with the signs and symptoms of bullying is that they could all be signs and symptoms of something else. They don't prove that bullying is taking place, they only indicate that it's a possibility. They might prompt you to try making some discreet enquiries among trusted teachers or the parents of your child's friends. But the only way that you can know for certain that your child is being bullied is by getting him to tell you about it himself.

Young children will often just come straight out with it. They are used to getting adults to sort out their problems for them, and they have more contact time with their teachers and parents so there are lots of opportunities for talking.

But older children are generally far less willing to tell anyone they're being bullied. They tend to feel that they ought to be able to sort it out on their own. They believe, often correctly, that their parents and teachers expect them to as well, and that therefore they'll be less willing to try and help. The bullying situation becomes a secret that they're too ashamed to share.

Shame is one of the reasons why your child might not want to tell you he's being bullied, but there are lots more.

SOME REASONS WHY YOUR CHILD MIGHT NOT WANT TO TALK ABOUT IT

1 Fear of reprisals

People who bully often use the threat of violence to stop their victims from telling anyone. Even when the bullying is purely verbal, children are usually afraid that it might escalate.

In schools which have not succeeded in creating a strong anti-bullying culture there is also the very real risk that telling will actually cause the bullying to spread.

This is how it works.

A child finds himself being bullied by some of the others in his class. He tells his teacher, and the bullies are punished. But word soon gets around the school that this child is an informer, and he starts to be taunted by people in other years as well as his own.

2 Ignorance

A lot of children don't understand that what is happening to them is bullying. Very young children may not even realize that hitting and kicking are wrong.

I remember, when my first child started school, feeling rather puzzled that besides her four or five best friends she wanted to invite one older boy to her birthday party. A week later I went to collect my child from someone else's party, and saw the same boy there as well.

'What's his secret?' I joked to another parent as we waited for the last party game to finish. 'Why do all these little girls seem to have taken such a shine to him?'

The parent laughed aloud. 'Oh, they don't like him,' he told me. 'They're frightened of him. Whenever anyone's giving out invitations at school he jumps on them and threatens to give them a good kicking if they don't give him one, too.'

My daughter confirmed this for me later, and I was really shocked. Why on earth hadn't she told me about it before?

'I just thought that was the way things were at big school,' she said.

Even much older children can fail to realize they are being bullied. I know a 13-year-old boy who was part of a well-established group of friends. When he fell out with one of them the whole group began to tease him. They pretended it was just in fun. The boy came to believe that not only was he fat and stupid, like they said, but he didn't have a sense of humour either because he was the only one who couldn't see the joke.

3 Resignation

Children often think that they are being picked on because there is actually something wrong with them. If it's a thing they can change, like wearing unfashionable clothes or coming top in tests, they'll probably try to do something about it.

This is usually a waste of time and they soon come to realize that whatever they do there's always something other children can tease them about. Then they join the ranks of people who are being taunted about something they obviously can't change, like the colour of their skin, and they can reach the conclusion that being picked on is something that they'll have to put up with for ever.

4 Denial

Many children who are persistently bullied can only cope by hoping against hope that if they just keep quiet and don't make too much fuss the whole thing will one day disappear all on its own.

■ 5 Fears about how you will react

The biggest fear most children have is that they won't be believed or that they won't be taken seriously, and this does happen very often, in fact, as in the case of Danny and Juliet (names have been changed to protect identities).

Danny and Juliet had to play together sometimes because their mothers were friends. Juliet was slightly older than Danny. She was angry at being stuck with him, and often felt bored. She amused herself by ruthlessly taunting and intimidating him. When Danny eventually complained to his mother she said she was sure Juliet didn't mean anything by it, and she told him off for getting worked up about a bit of harmless fun.

Your child might also be afraid that you'll react by:

- taking the whole matter out of his hands, and deciding on a course of action without getting his agreement
- criticizing him for getting into such a bad situation in the first place, or for not being able to sort it out for himself
- offering him advice he can't take, like 'Just tell a teacher' or 'Pretend you don't care', which will only make him feel worse
- getting angry
- getting upset

Before you decide to ask your child whether he is being bullied, take a few moments to think about the powerful reasons he might have for holding back. Feel the emotions. Then, if he refuses to talk about it or if he admits he is being bullied but won't go into detail, you'll be less tempted to badger him. Trying to force him to open up about it will probably just make him even more reluctant to do so.

Have patience. Bullying is usually a situation rather than an event, and it's a situation your child has probably been in for a while if he's showing signs of distress. He'll cope for a couple more days while you set your mind on how to create the sort of conditions that will make your child feel it's safe to talk.

▓ HELPING YOUR CHILD TO FEEL IT'S SAFE TO TALK

The first thing to think about is whether you actually have enough space for talking in your day-to-day life. Most of us don't have a lot of spare time and while some families are comfortable with setting aside a special time for conversation, over a family meal for instance, many others would find this artificial and embarrassing.

You don't have to drop everything and talk to each other all the time, but you do need to make it clear to your child that you are available if he wants to talk, and this means, of course, that you must actually be prepared to take a break if he wants you to and give him your full attention.

So, when your child comes into the room, stop what you are doing for a few seconds, look up at him and make a few opening remarks. He can then choose whether to stay and talk or go off and do something else.

If he stays, you will have an opportunity to work on the next thing you might like to consider – how do you talk to your child? Do you joke a lot? Do you tend to tease him? To disbelieve or belittle him? To patronize him? Do you talk about other people in disparaging ways? Simply noticing the sort of things you say can bring some big surprises.

Some years ago I was telling my family rather scornfully about a book I was reading in which one of the exercises was to go for a whole hour without criticizing anyone. 'How ridiculous!' I scoffed. 'Anyone could do that.' To my surprise and consternation, they challenged me to try. I lasted four and a half minutes. So now, not scornfully – not critically! – I recommend this exercise to you.

There are so many oblique ways of being critical. 'Seventy-six per cent? That's excellent! Just think what you could have got if you had revised more . . .'

'Your room's looking tidy for a change . . .'

'I think I'd better do that for you . . .'

'What a nice colour – though, of course, I wouldn't have chosen it myself . . .'

The key to avoiding being critical and judgemental is to focus on feelings. When you are talking focus on your own feelings, and when your child is talking focus on his. For instance, instead of saying, 'My boss was being a pain in the neck today,' you could say, 'I got really fed up with my boss today . . .'.

If your child tells you that he didn't do as well as he'd expected in his science test you might be tempted to say, 'Never mind, it doesn't matter,' but that would be your feeling, not his. You might say, 'That's awful! What went wrong?' but that would be your feeling, too. Try saying you can see he feels disappointed; you know he expected to do well; you imagine it could really have spoilt his day.

Listening with empathy is a skill that comes more easily to some people than to others. If you find it difficult, don't worry. Counsellors have to do special training to get the hang of it, and working at it on your own takes time. Just bear in mind that it's an option and use it when you remember to, which will often be when you've caught yourself saying something particularly judgemental.

Focusing on your child's feelings will be particularly helpful when he finally plucks up the courage to talk about what's really troubling him because, when he offers you a clue, you won't miss it.

The clue could be something like this:

Your child – 'I've got a sore leg.'
You – 'Oh? How did that happen?'
Your child – 'Jamie tripped me up in football.'
You – 'Was it an accident, do you think?'
Your child shakes his head.

At this point, any of these responses will close the conversation down again:

- 'The little swine! I'll knock his block off when I see him!'
- 'Where was your teacher, then? She really ought to deal with that kid!'

- 'Oh, dear! How could anybody be so horrible? I mean, I just don't understand it . . .'

If you want to encourage him to go on, empathize with him. This means validating his feelings and helping him to clarify them. It puts you on the same team.

You – 'I bet you felt pretty annoyed about that . . .'
Your child – 'I did. I got cross, and then they all started laughing at me.'
You – 'That must've been really embarrassing.'
Your child – 'Actually, they keep on doing it . . .'

When he's ready, and not before, the whole truth will come out, and you can help your child enormously if you believe what he tells you, acknowledge his feelings and refrain from judging or belittling him.

■ WHEN THE TRUTH COMES OUT

As the details emerge you may well feel shocked, horrified, fearful and furious by turns or, of course, you may feel that he's making a big fuss about nothing. Either way, if you can stay focused on his emotions you're less likely to get carried away by your own.

You might be tempted to try to avoid the uncomfortable business of talking about such difficult things by taking action straight away or giving your child lots of advice and instructions, but this would not be in your child's best interests. What he needs in the first instance is not a champion or a teacher – he needs a witness.

Giving him a safe space to talk about what's happening to him will be helping him in three important ways. First, it will mean he's no longer having to keep a secret, and secrets attract guilt and shame like jam attracts bluebottles. Second, it will enable him to release some of his pent-up emotions, and when strong emotions are bottled up they become even more dangerous because you never know when they might explode. Last, but not least, it will show him that you are committed to helping him to sort out the problem without disregarding his feelings and opinions or trying to take over.

Explain to your child that talking about problems is important as an end in itself, whether solutions emerge out of it or not. Tell him how beneficial it is to let your feelings out. Suggest that if it's too hard for him to tell you all the details, and he doesn't want to tell a friend or teacher or another family member, he might like to phone a helpline and talk to one of their counsellors. He might even tell his dog or his rabbit – they can certainly be relied upon not to overwhelm him with advice.

Ask him if he'd like to write it all down in a diary. That will not only allow him to express his most painful feelings, but also provide an accurate record if he decides later on to involve the authorities. Quite often the children who have been doing the bullying are full of remorse when they actually see the facts written down on paper and read about the destructive effects their actions have had.

Finally, don't forget to praise your child for managing to talk about it, and to congratulate yourself on being able to help him.

Your child can't begin to get to grips with his situation until he is able to talk about it, and you can't begin to help him until you know the facts. Opening a dialogue is the first, and sometimes the most difficult, step. Keeping it open as things progress will also be very important.

For your child, talking is a way of freeing himself from shame, getting a more objective perspective and facing up to the fact that he has a problem. Having you listen is a way of feeling less alone.

When you both know exactly what is going on, you can sit down together and work out what you want to do about it.

Chapter Two

Approaching the School

If your child is being bullied by other children at her own school, the first thing you'll have to consider is whether to ask the school to take action. Interestingly, when you're thinking about telling the school what is going on you might find yourself holding back for all the same reasons that children hold back from telling their parents.

You might feel ashamed that your child has a problem, or if she's always been picked on you might think it's just something she'll have to learn to live with. You might want to ignore it and hope it'll go away on its own. You might be afraid the teachers will not believe you, or suggest you're overreacting, or take over and decide what to do without consulting you. You'll almost certainly feel worried that any action the school takes could make things worse for your child instead of better.

These are all perfectly reasonable fears. Parents who complain that their children are being bullied are frequently perceived as being over-protective, especially if the bullying is non-physical, and sometimes intervention by the school really does make matters worse.

So when you are considering whether to approach the school listen to what your child has to say about it. She's the expert. She knows how things are normally done, and her perceptions can tell you much more about the ethos of the school than any written policy document. What she has to say will not only help you to decide whether to go and talk about it but also what kind of reception to expect when you do.

However, if your child is extremely reluctant to inform the school, or if she has already done so to no avail, try not to let yourself be overcome by her fear and despondency. Even when effective action and advice is not forthcoming, opening a dialogue with the school can be very helpful. It is empowering for you and your child to express your feelings about the situation, and it disperses the unwholesome atmosphere of secrecy.

Reassure your child that she will be present at any meeting you arrange. Explain that you will not allow the school to take any action she does not agree with. But tell her that in certain circumstances it is almost always worth taking the risk and telling the school, especially when the bullying is physical.

PHYSICAL BULLYING: WHY IT'S A GOOD IDEA TO INFORM THE SCHOOL

Physical bullying always involves acts that outside school would be illegal. Schools have a legal duty of care for all their pupils, and they have to take every report of physical bullying seriously. You are not likely to be patronized or palmed off if you tell the school that your child is being physically bullied.

The illegal nature of physical bullying makes the question of punishment of offenders very straightforward, and most schools have effective disciplinary procedures that will come into play as soon as physical bullying is proven.

Incidents of physical bullying are easier to identify and prove than non-physical forms, and situations of physical bullying are easier to monitor. Some schools use closed circuit television as well as adult supervision in the playground. Children who witness physical assaults can be in no doubt about what's going on, and some schools offer bully-boxes and other discreet ways of informing.

Furthermore, although I have heard some teachers take a 'boys will be boys' attitude about playground violence, most people feel that physical assault is always unacceptable. Children who bully in physical ways put themselves automatically in the wrong, and their victims are therefore usually assured of sympathy and support.

Informing the school about physical bullying can feel risky, but the alternatives are generally worse. Just leaving it and hoping it will go away on its own is likely to result in an escalation of violence, with your child becoming progressively less capable of defending herself psychologically or physically. Expecting your child to tackle the people who are pushing her around is un-realistic because most bullying involves groups of people picking on one weaker child, and some of them may even be carrying weapons. Besides, if your child did try to retaliate she might well find that she got into trouble for bullying herself.

Taking the matter into your own hands by confronting the children who are bullying yours can be effective if they are quite young, but it is more often a recipe for disaster. I have seen school problems develop into feuds that involved whole families when the parents got directly involved. So go carefully on this one, and trust your intuition.

Moving school might give your child some respite, but it can also make matters worse because often the problem follows the child, and she will then have to deal with the stress of moving as well as a fresh burst of bullying.

If the situation is very serious, or if your child has already tried several different schools, you might consider taking her out of school altogether. This is a growing trend, and need not result in any loss of academic achievement. But it isn't a step that most parents have the time, the money or the confidence to take and, like moving schools, it has one major drawback – it avoids the issue rather than tackling it. Children who manage to stay put, to have faith in themselves and their teachers and to develop the inner resources they need to cope with the bullying situation can feel much better about themselves than those who feel they have had to run away.

So, if your child is being bullied physically, see if she will agree to you setting up a meeting with her class teacher, head of year or the senior teacher with responsibility for student welfare and discipline. Make sure your child is involved. Even if the school is already aware of the problem, discussing it in this three-way manner will show your child that you support her one hundred per cent, and let the school know that you are willing to do whatever you can to help.

▪ STARTING A DIALOGUE

How you approach your first meeting with the school will determine how productive it is. If you allow your upset and angry feelings to take over, and adopt a confrontational attitude, you will probably only succeed in making your child more anxious and her teacher more defensive.

The best way to contain your own feelings is by trying to empathize with those of the teacher. Bear in mind that she may also feel upset and angry about a child in her care being hurt and intimidated. She may feel responsible, or she may feel that she is being made responsible for problems that originate outside school, which families and communities are failing to address themselves. She may be struggling to cope with a number of severely disturbed individuals in a large class with little or no extra support. She will certainly be aware that there's no easy solution.

In this meeting, try to stay focused on three main aims – to establish the facts, have your feelings acknowledged and agree a plan of action.

▪ 1 Establishing the facts

It is helpful if you can provide accurate dates, times and places for any bullying incidents you want to discuss, along with the names of all the children present, even those who were not actively involved. This will be much easier if you and your child have kept a written record of events.

However, if your child really doesn't want to name names she shouldn't have to. Making the school aware that there is a problem in a general way is enough for them to be able to address it in a general way. It also alerts staff to the fact that your child may be at risk so that they can be more vigilant.

2　Having your feelings acknowledged

You have a right to be listened to, and to have your concerns taken seriously. Don't be palmed off with platitudes. Be perfectly clear that whatever goes on outside school, inside school all social and behavioural matters are the school's responsibility. It is up to the school to take action, but if you are not happy about what sort of action is proposed your reservations should be respected.

3　Agreeing a plan of action

Most schools will have procedures for checking the facts when bullying is reported, and these might include interviewing everyone involved together or separately and getting written statements from the main players.

Once bullying is established, almost all schools will deal with it by punishing the ones doing the bullying and supporting the ones being bullied. Punishments can range from detentions to permanent exclusion. Support might include providing a named member of staff that your child can go and see if she feels worried, or some form of counselling.

You might well feel it's perverse to offer counselling to your child instead of to the children whose uncontrolled aggression is what is causing all the problems, and in some enlightened schools the bullying child is perceived as the one who needs help and support. But your child might want to accept the offer so don't be too quick to dismiss it on her behalf.

In fact, whatever your gut reaction to the measures the school suggests, try to bear in mind that they are dealing with problems like this all the time. They will probably have tried lots of different styles of punishment and support, and decided what works best for them.

Once you have agreed in principle what action should be taken, ask specifically what will be done to protect your child from any repercussions, and arrange a follow-up meeting to discuss how things are going.

▮ WHAT HAPPENS NEXT

This depends on the individual circumstances as well as the school's normal procedures, but any action the school takes should be quick and decisive.

Here's an example.

Adam

Twelve-year-old Adam was picked on mercilessly by a group of boys in his class who called him names, kicked his chair, spat on his work and poked him with rulers in most of his lessons. Things got out of hand one day when the teacher was out of the room and Adam was punched and kicked in front of the whole class. His parents complained.

Their first meeting was with Adam's head of year. He immediately interviewed every child in Adam's class individually, and identified the two main culprits. He arranged meetings with them and their parents, and agreed punishments. One of the boys was excluded from school for a week and the other was put on report and ordered to attend three further meetings between his parents and the head of year to monitor his behaviour.

Adam was offered a place in a support group of 'vulnerable children', which he declined on the grounds that he didn't want to be singled out as odd or inadequate.

The head of year then talked to the whole class about the incident, encouraging them to feel empathy for Adam and to take responsibility for their part in what happened. Many of them subsequently apologized to him.

Adam's parents met the head of year a few days later, and were able to confirm that all the physical bullying had stopped. They met him again after a month. The physical bullying had not resumed but Adam was being teased for telling, and they discussed ways of helping him to handle this.

IF NOTHING HAPPENS

If after a day or two nothing seems to have been done or if you are unhappy about your initial meeting, ask to see the head-teacher. Again try to adopt a non-confrontational attitude, establish the facts, have your feelings acknowledged and agree a plan of action.

If this meeting is unsatisfactory, or if there seems to be no follow-up, your next recourse is to the school governors or whatever authority administers the school. Many parents feel most comfortable talking to a parent-governor, but any of them will do.

After that, if you are still not satisfied, try making a written complaint to the head-teacher, chair of governors or the governing body in question, giving all the facts and asking them to send you a plan of action in writing.

Who you contact next will depend on what type of school it is and in which country you live. In the UK, the following is the procedure: for an LEA school, complaints should be addressed to the Director of Education; for a church school, the diocese and for a grant-maintained school the Secretary of State.

If all else fails, parents can take legal action, but fortunately it very rarely comes to this. Most schools do cope with incidents of physical bullying, even if it means shifting the problem outside school by expelling the children concerned.

Non-physical bullying, on the other hand, is different.

WHY NON-PHYSICAL BULLYING IS DIFFERENT

Physical aggression can be controlled in school, as it is in the community, by good policing and effective punishments. But non-physical bullying is not about rules and laws – it's about values.

Teasing, excluding, whispering campaigns and so on are not against the law, and people who engage in them can easily think that they are not doing anything wrong. This makes the whole issue of punishment less cut and dried, and if the bully can't be punished it's easy for the victim to come to be seen as the problem.

In addition to this, many teachers still regard non-physical bullying as comparatively trivial, and can feel antagonistic towards people who don't share this view. Some teachers may even go so far as to publicly humiliate children who complain of being teased.

All in all, if you decide to inform your child's school about non-physical bullying there is quite a high chance that either no action will be taken or such action as is taken will actually make matters worse. Whether you decide to take the risk will depend upon your impression of the school, your assessment of the situation and how your child feels about it.

On the whole, it's usually a good idea to open a dialogue, if only because it helps the teachers to know what's going on, and you can always ask them not to intervene directly. You will need to be particularly clear in your objectives and unwavering in your support for your child because you are very likely to come up against attitudes like these:

■ **'This school doesn't have a problem with bullying . . .'**
(Subtext: 'You're the one with the problem.')

Bullying is a fact of life. 'This school doesn't have a problem with bullying' means 'This school doesn't care about bullying'.

■ **'It's not exactly serious, is it – a bit of teasing and name-calling?'**
(Subtext: 'You're making a big fuss about nothing.')

Cuts and bruises heal, but sustained attacks on a person's self-image can have devastating effects in every area of her life. Studies show that non-physical bullying leaves emotional scars that are more painful and long-lasting than physical forms.

In tribal communities, exclusion from the group is considered a more terrifying punishment than death. Non-physical bullying can drive children to despair. A few may resort to suicide, or suffer such a build-up of anger and hatred that they are driven to retaliate with uncharacteristic violence.

Most children rightly fear that verbal bullying can lead on to physical bullying if it is allowed to go unchecked.

▓ **'It's no good trying to protect children from the normal cut and thrust of life . . .'**
(Subtext: 'You're an over-protective parent and your child is too sensitive.')

This is nonsense. Some teasing is normal in life, but very few people indeed have to go to their place of work day after day knowing they'll be insulted and abused continuously, called names, spat on and universally despised. Very few people face being ostracized by all their colleagues all the time.

Anyone who complains about such treatment is not being over-sensitive – he's sticking up for his right to enjoy a normal degree of civility and respect.

▓ **'Boys will be boys . . .' and 'Girls will be girls . . .'**
(Subtext: 'Your child isn't a proper girl [boy] if she [he] can't accept behaviour natural to her [his] gender.')

Sexual stereotypes are no more an excuse for bullying in childhood than in adult life. We don't say 'Men will be men' and therefore brawl and beat their wives, and we don't say 'Women will be women' and therefore spread vicious rumours and slander.

▓ **'This group may be high-spirited, but I wouldn't say they were bullies . . .'**
(Subtext: 'Your child is lying.')

If at first you aren't believed, keep insisting until you are. The hardest part is telling someone for the first time – after that, it gets much easier.

■ 'Your child is a bit of a loner . . .'
(Subtext: 'Your child is maladjusted and immature: she needs to change and be more sociable.')

Sociability is not a measure of maturity, it's a feature of personality. Trying to force a quiet child who is happy in her own company to become more sociable and outgoing is about as sensible as trying to make a clever child slow, or a slow child clever.

It devalues her gift of self-sufficiency and can make her feel there's something fundamentally wrong with her.

All these attitudes condone bullying and put the bullied child at fault, and if you can counter them calmly and clearly your child will feel wonderfully supported and reassured.

You will gain insights into how much help the staff will be able to offer your child by simply noticing how you yourself feel after the meeting. If you feel blamed or criticized, ignored or belittled, that's how your child will feel when she tells. If you feel a sense of concern, co-operation and commitment, she will feel it, too.

Of course, there are schools that take non-physical bullying very seriously and deal with it effectively, but I haven't mentioned them yet because it seems to me that if your child attends such a school she will probably be quite happy to sort things out with her teachers, and not involve you at all.

I heard a lovely story a couple of weeks ago which perfectly illustrates this:

Emily
My husband, who is a head-teacher, told us about an eight-year-old girl who came to his office to complain that two other girls in her class had been teasing her and making her cry. (Names have been changed to protect the identities of people concerned.)

He brought the three girls together to talk about it. First, he asked the two who were teasing if they knew why he had asked them to come.

'It's because we've been teasing Emily, isn't it?' said one.

'That's right,' my husband agreed. 'And it's making Emily feel very unhappy. What do you think we could do about it?'

The two little girls looked at each other, and then they looked at Emily. Suddenly, one of them piped up, 'Well . . . we *could* stop teasing her!'

They both decided to write letters of apology to Emily, and the teasing stopped.

That wasn't quite the end of the story, though. When one of the parents saw her daughter writing her letter of apology she went straight to the school to complain that my husband had accused her child of bullying. It's just as well she took the child with her.

'But I *was* bullying!' the child protested, when she heard what her mother had to say.

If only things always went as smoothly as that!

The problem is that a really effective anti-bullying policy requires a lot of commitment from the whole school community. It takes time and energy to create a strong ethos built on respect and civility, and it can also take money for training if some teachers are using sarcasm, ridicule and shouting to control their classes, for example, or some lunchtime supervisors favour turning a blind eye. Values can't be taught or legislated for – they have to be learned by example.

Individual incidents of non-physical bullying can only be dealt with effectively in a school environment that wholly disapproves of all forms of bullying. Not allowing even the least serious offences to go unchallenged seems to cause a reduction in more serious offences too.

But you have to be pragmatic. Although there are effective programmes like the 'no blame approach' available to schools for creating a strong ethos against bullying, there is no quick-fix solution, and you have to work with the system as it is in your child's school right now.

If you don't feel confident that your child can be helped in direct ways by the school, see if there are any indirect ways they could help her. Providing somewhere safe for her to go at lunch-times, reorganizing the classroom so that she never has to sit next to her tormentors or making sure that teachers arrive for lessons on time are all small things that could make a big difference.

On the whole, it's probably a good idea to inform the school if your child is being bullied, especially if the bullying is partly physical, but don't expect the school to work miracles. Bullying is a complex problem that is deeply rooted in society.

Your child has a legal right to physical protection, and she will have it. But it's much harder for schools to protect their pupils from teasing and name-calling and the psychological damage they can cause.

Fortunately, your child can learn to protect herself from being hurt by bullying, and you are in an ideal position to help her.

Chapter Three

Helping Your Child to Help Himself

The problem with most of the conventional advice to children who are being bullied is that it focuses on the child's behaviour instead of on his feelings. If he feels bad about himself and tries to act as if he doesn't, no one will be taken in by it, least of all himself. Besides, that would be concealing the problem rather than solving it. But if he feels good about himself his behaviour will change automatically.

Emotions are the key to all forms of bullying. Making other people feel bad is the pay-off for those who bully. For those who are bullied, the feelings of rage, anxiety and helplessness, as well as the consequent loss of confidence and self-esteem, are far more damaging than any physical effects, and will often last long after the actual bullying has stopped.

Many people think you can't change the way you feel, but you can. Your child can turn the victim feelings of rage, anxiety and helplessness into detachment, confidence and power by changing the way he perceives the situation, developing a positive attitude, building up his self-esteem and learning constructive ways of dealing with anger and fear.

These are simple skills to master, as I shall be showing in the remaining chapters of this book, and you are in an ideal position to help your child because you will be experiencing exactly the same feelings in relation to the bullying situation as he is.

You can do the work together, and you don't have to do it on your own.

■ YOU ARE NOT ALONE

All the ideas in this book will be easier and more fun if the whole family joins in with them. You don't necessarily need to tell everyone the reason why you're thinking about making the house a blame-free zone, creating a positive environment, and so on, if you think that it might draw attention to your bullied child's problems in an unhelpful way. You might prefer to present the whole thing as an interesting experiment. Young children will be quite happy to treat it all like a game, and older children, who are becoming aware of different lifestyle choices, are usually curious to try anything new.

Explain what you are doing, and invite anyone who wants to join in. Make it clear that nobody has to if he doesn't want to. Congratulate yourself and each other when it goes right, and support yourself and each other when you find yourselves backsliding.

Even if some members of your family don't want to take an active part in the process they can help by listening to what you have to say about it and understanding what you are trying to do.

Your friends can help in the same way, by being sounding-boards for the ideas you're working with. Naturally, they may not agree – I'm sure several of my friends and my children's probably thought we'd all gone a bit peculiar at times when we began to work in this way. But talking will help you to get things clear in your own mind and besides, your friends might have some good ideas of their own to contribute about making positive change.

Who else can help? Well, you can sometimes gain strength by sharing ideas with people who understand what you are going through, and if you know of other parents whose children are having problems at school it might be a good idea to set up an informal support group. This could be a good forum for talking about self-help ideas, so long as it isn't allowed to degenerate into a place where everyone goes just to grumble and complain about the school.

Finally, you could always book a couple of sessions with a counsellor. A lot of people have a strong resistance to the very idea of counselling because they believe it shows you're either crazy or inadequate if you need it. That's a great pity because all it actually shows is that you're able to acknowledge a problem and determined to sort it out.

Talking always helps, and counsellors are trained to listen without being judgemental or interfering. A counsellor could be particularly useful to you if you decide to work through the ideas in this book because he will be familiar with the concepts and used to working in this sort of way.

You could see a counsellor on your own or with your child, whichever feels better. Many health centres can provide counselling services, or at least tell you where you can get private counselling locally. Fees are often negotiable, depending on your ability to pay. There are various telephone helplines which offer counselling to parents as well as children (*see* Useful Addresses, p. 102).

All these people can help you if you want them to, so do bear that in mind as you and your child tackle the first great challenge of any self-help programme – letting go of blame.

▒ LETTING GO OF BLAME

It's quite common for everyone involved in the bullying situation to blame somebody else. You might blame your own child or the child who is bullying him, his teachers or even society in general. Your child might blame the bullying child, his school or you for not being able to sort it out. His teachers might blame all or any of the children involved and all or any of the parents.

The problem is that while everyone is just sitting around blaming somebody else, no one's actually doing something about it. Blame makes you passive. Saying, 'It's not my fault,' is the same as saying, 'I can't do anything about it,' or perhaps even, 'Why should I?'

If you want to take a more active and powerful position you have to let go of blame and accept responsibility.

■ RESPONSE-ABILITY IS POWER

However much you feel that someone else is to blame, there's nothing you can say or do to them that will force them to change their behaviour, and this can leave you feeling helpless and frustrated.

But although you can't force other people to change the way they behave, you can change the way you respond and, interestingly, changing how you respond to other people is the most effective way of changing how they behave towards you.

I learnt this important lesson some years ago when my children were small, and my husband and I were in the throes of a long-running argument about his irregular working hours. I wanted him to organize his work so that he came home at roughly the same time each day, and I became angry that he was always naming a time and never sticking to it.

I felt he was being irresponsible, he felt I was being un-reasonable – and that was where we were stuck. The way through the impasse was for me to back off and stop trying to make him do what I wanted. I stopped making arrangements that depended on him being home, and just let it go. Pretty soon it really didn't matter to me any more that he should regulate his working hours – and then, of course, he did.

You can test out for yourself how changing your responses to other people changes the way they behave towards you. Supposing you always pass the same person on the way to work. He always ignores you so you ignore him. Try saying a cheerful hello. Keep it up for a couple of days. Is he still ignoring you? Supposing someone at work often gets stressed and shouts at you so you shout back. Stop shouting. Keep it up for a couple of days. Is she still shouting at you?

These are obvious examples, but getting people to change by

changing how you respond can work in more mysterious ways. Does someone you know have a habit that really annoys you? If you stop reacting with annoyance two interesting things happen. First, it stops bothering you and, next, it stops.

If your child can stop caring about the teasing and name-calling, the teasing and name-calling will stop. But the only way he can begin to stop caring is by taking responsibility for his own emotions. This means shifting the focus from 'them' – 'They're making me feel bad' and 'They're frightening me' – to 'me'. 'I'm letting them make me feel bad' and 'I'm letting them frighten me'.

You can't make him take responsibility by telling him to, but in this, as in all other areas, you can get the change you want in him by making changes in yourself. If you can change your own behaviour, and explain what you are doing, you will set an example of blame-free attitudes that will soon rub off on him.

CREATING A BLAME-FREE ZONE

Letting go of blame in the bullying situation is a particularly hard thing to do because bullying is obviously wrong, the person who bullies is obviously the cause of this wrong and the situation is extremely painful.

It will be easier to approach the idea of letting go of blame in a more general way at first by making your household a blame-free zone. A simple and effective way to start is by banning the 'b' word and the 'f' word.

The 'b' word and the 'f' word

In our family, the 'b' word is 'blame' and the 'f' word is 'fault', and they are as unacceptable as the other 'b' and 'f' words.

If you ban these words you will instantly become aware of all the ways we imply blame without naming it, and that will help you to notice and root out any implications of blame.

For example, imagine you're washing up and your child is

grumbling about having to dry. You break a plate. Your first impulse might be to say, 'That was your fault for making me feel stressed out!' If you have to avoid the 'f' word you might say instead, 'Look what you've made me do!' or 'I wouldn't have done that if you hadn't been giving me so much earache!'. But if you let go of even the implication of blame then you have no choice but to take responsibility – the fact is, it was you who broke the plate.

'Fault' and 'blame' are the tip of the iceberg which draws your attention to what's underneath. Here are some other subtle ways you might notice yourself shifting responsibility onto your child –

* *You're making me worried/angry/unhappy . . .*
  It's up to you how you feel so just say, 'I feel worried/ angry/unhappy.'
* *You mustn't upset your father/mother/grandmother . . .*
  It's up to father/mother/grandmother how they feel so don't be tempted to use them as a lever. There's no need to bring them into it at all.
* *I can't cope if you don't behave . . .*
  Your ability to cope should not depend on your child making things easy for you. Accept his behaviour, like any other challenge life presents you with. You wouldn't say, 'I can't cope if I get flu/have an accident/burn the dinner . . .' because there would be no point. No one else can protect you from these difficulties. Don't ask your child to protect you from the normal challenges of being a parent. Whether you can cope or not depends entirely on you.
* *You're being difficult . . .*
  If you find your child difficult, that's your problem, not his. So say, 'I'm finding your behaviour difficult' instead.

As you begin to take conscious responsibility for your own feelings, your child will also start to take responsibility for his. Being responsible is far less comfortable than blaming someone else, and you will make if much easier for him if you resist the temptation to protect him.

You may think, for instance, that you're being understanding and sympathetic by taking the attitude that he's bound to feel upset by the bullying situation, that he's perfectly normal and it's not his problem. But trying to comfort your child in this way will only make his response to the situation seem inevitable, and discourage him from feeling empowered to change it.

It may seen harsh to tell your child that he's letting the children who are bullying him make him feel angry and frightened, but it's actually a way of helping him to take control.

As you start to notice all the ways you shift blame onto other people you will also notice all the ways they try to shift blame onto you. The glorious up-side to letting go of blame is that you also find yourself breaking free of guilt.

After all, if it's up to you how you choose to respond to other people, it's surely up to them how they choose to respond to you. As soon as you stop thinking it's your child's fault when you feel irritable and upset, you'll also stop thinking it's your fault when he does.

It takes persistence and determination, but most of all it takes clear thinking if you want to stop blaming other people for your bad feelings and not let them blame you. Picturing bad feelings as something concrete getting passed around from one person to another can help you to be more aware of what's going on.

When anyone tries to dump their bad feelings on me I find it helpful to visualize their anger, resentment, jealousy or whatever it is as a hot potato. I'm sorry they're finding it too hot to handle, but I don't hesitate to give it back.

THE GAME OF HOT POTATOES

Your child can think of bullying as a game of hot potatoes. He can see the bully as a person with bad feelings he can't handle. He only needs to notice his own feelings to realize that you don't even think of hurting other people when you feel happy – it's only when you feel bad that you need someone to take it out on.

It may be hard to understand why your child's tormentor is

feeling bad because children who bully don't fit any stereotype of deprivation and abuse. Children from successful, wealthy backgrounds can have less obvious pressures to bear, like the weight of unrealistic parental ambitions, for example, or negative undercurrents in their family relationships.

Often, there are clues in the nature of the bullying. A girl who feels anxious about her body shape might tease someone else for being fat. If she can make her victim start to worry about her body shape then the bad feeling is precisely transferred.

A boy who wants to work hard and achieve well but is afraid of being teased for his keenness might tease someone else for being too keen. If he can make his victim feel worried about working hard and doing well then the bad feeling is precisely transferred.

Even quite young children can easily grasp this concept. I was talking to an eight-year-old recently who had been teased all summer for having fat legs, and this had made her too embarrassed to wear shorts and skirts. When I explained to her about the hot potatoes, she thought for a few moments and then remarked that she had, in fact, noticed that the girl who teased her always wore long trousers herself.

From then on this child wore shorts. When I saw her again I asked if she was still being teased.

'Oh, no,' she told me. 'I talked to that girl on her own, and told her I was sorry she felt she had fat legs, but personally I thought they were just fine!'

Sometimes the hot potato gets passed around, with the bullied child taking out his anger and anxiety on someone else so that he becomes a bully, too. Very often a child who doesn't dare to express his anger and frustration at school will let it all out in the comparative safety of his home. If your child does this to you he will be giving you the perfect opportunity to show him how to refuse to be bullied by giving the hot potato back.

Imagine that your child has been teased at school about his coat. As soon as he gets home he starts shouting at you for buying him the wrong sort of coat and demanding that you go straight out and get him a new one.

You would be fully justified in feeling angry, hurt and bewildered by this unprovoked attack, but that would be giving your child a model of victim attitudes and doubling the level of anxiety and anger in the situation.

It would be much better to acknowledge your child's bad feelings, but make it perfectly clear that those feelings belong to him. Not allowing him to make you angry and upset means you will be able to feel sympathetic towards him rather than resentful. What's more, he will feel safer because his bad feelings are contained, and he won't have to carry any extra burden of guilt.

A simple technique for giving the hot potato back is called 'fogging'. This is an invaluable skill for anyone who often has to cope with other people's aggression. It just means putting up a smokescreen to conceal your own views and values by appearing to agree with your aggressor. 'You could be right', 'Thank you for pointing that out', 'I'll certainly give this some thought' and so on are great ways of defusing aggression. Keeping your own opinion hidden means you don't take anything personally, or feel the need to retaliate.

Giving the hot potato back is not about retaliation. It's about refusing to be involved in someone else's problem. Being clear that people who bully have a problem makes it easier to let go of blame.

Although the problem is often to do with bad feelings, it can sometimes come from a lack of good feelings, like kindness and concern. A child who seems popular and well adjusted, and has no particular urge to hurt anyone, can behave in hurtful ways because he simply lacks empathy. Small children are very self-centred, and they have to learn how to be sociable by becoming aware of other people's feelings. Children who bully because they lack empathy have failed to mature in this way. They will find it difficult to make healthy relationships, and so to develop a strong self-image.

Other children, who don't have problems with aggression or empathy, may become involved in bullying because they lack self-confidence. These children are so desperate to belong or so afraid of becoming victims that they are willing to put their own moral scruples on one side in order to co-operate with a bullying gang. They will be particularly vulnerable to peer pressure in other areas such as drinking, smoking and drugs.

Seeing people who bully as having a problem can help us to be less blameful. Here are some more ways of avoiding blame.

MORE WAYS OF AVOIDING BLAME

1 Accept that nobody's perfect

We all indulge in bullying behaviour from time to time. Everyone sometimes takes out their bad mood on someone else; everyone says tactless and hurtful things, and everyone will occasionally be willing to exclude people who do not fit in with their friendship group. Not being blameful when other people do it means not having to feel guilty when you do it yourself.

2 Don't label

Labelling children as 'victims' and 'bullies' means identifying the problem as something wrong with them rather than their behaviour. It ignores the other aspects of their personality – the caring side, the powerful side – that will enable them to alter their behaviour, and so it removes the feeling that they are capable of change.

It can be helpful to avoid labelling people generally. 'You're a naughty boy' is more crushing and negative than 'That was a naughty thing to do', for instance. 'Your teacher is hopeless' is more judgemental than 'Your teacher doesn't seem to have handled that incident well'.

3 Don't judge

Demonizing the child who is bullying yours is not a good idea. People on both sides of the bullying relationship can feel better about themselves by denigrating the other. Just as the one who bullies can feel stronger, braver and more in control because he sees his victim as weak, cowardly and at his mercy, so the one who is bullied can feel that he holds the moral high ground if he sees the bully as wicked and wrong. He may risk becoming one of those people in life who would rather be right than happy.

4 Ask yourself, 'How else might this situation serve my child?'

Being a victim could have other pay-offs besides making your child feel good and innocent in contrast to the bad, guilty person who is bullying him.

If he has poor self-esteem, for example, it can reinforce his low opinion of himself. This may not seem like much of a pay-off, but the fact is that however sad or self-limiting their world-view, people feel reassured by things that support it and threatened by things that contradict it. So if your child's experience of himself is as someone who doesn't deserve to be liked, being bullied could feel entirely appropriate to him. If he's very self-critical, other critical voices will simply validate his own.

Other pay-offs to consider are that if your child is stressed by any aspect of school life, bullying might give him a welcome excuse for going to ground, and if he has worries or difficulties outside school it might create a distraction.

It's hard to accept that such a horrible situation could have some pay-off for your child, but it's worth considering it if you can. Look at the effects of the bullying on your child and your family. Is it making him a focus of attention? Is it distracting you from the new baby/job/house/redundancy/divorce?

Your child did not consciously ask to be bullied, but if it has pay-offs for him that you don't address it will be harder for him to break out of it.

Letting go of blame means not waiting for someone else to change, but being ready to sort things out for yourself. It's a wonderfully empowering thing to do.

But how can your child actually go on to sort out such an alarming problem as bullying? How can he start to feel good about himself again? How can he ever stop feeling frightened and intimidated, or cope with such an intensity of rage?

The answer is that he can't do it all straight away. He's like a mile-a-day jogger who has decided to run a marathon – he will need to build up his general fitness first.

The fitness your child needs to combat his self-doubt, fear and anger is not physical. He needs to build up his inner resourcefulness, and you can help him to do this by creating a really positive home environment.

Chapter Four

Creating a Positive Environment

Even the most robust and optimistic child can have her confidence in herself and her world worn down by persistent bullying. Even the most successful parent can begin to fall prey to self-doubt, and question his past behaviour and his future ability to cope. The whole family can find itself on a downward spiral of negative and catastrophic thinking that flushes away all its energy and resourcefulness like water disappearing down a plug-hole.

Positive thinking is the plug!

The idea of positive thinking is that your experience of life depends not on what happens to you but on how you interpret it. So life is not something you suffer – it's something you create.

Positive thinking is an attitude of mind that is active rather than passive, and that makes it a step in the right direction for anyone stuck in the bullying situation.

If you haven't come across positive thinking before, you will probably have your doubts about it at first. It does seem to involve a lot of denial, and you may feel that it requires you to turn your back on the harsh realities of life. But it's easy and interesting, so why not give it a go? My children wanted to join in too, but if yours don't, it doesn't really matter. Positive thinking is catching – if one person gets it the rest of the family soon come down with it, like flu!

There are four main areas to think about: positive words, positive thoughts, positive feelings and positive lifestyle.

In our family, we started with positive words.

▒ POSITIVE WORDS

The positive approach to language turns conventional thinking on its head – it sees language not as describing experience but as creating it. It reverses the normal sequence of Be–Think–Say, and proposes a new sequence of Say–Think–Be.

For example, supposing a man says he has a good job. We might assume he says it because he thinks it, and he thinks it because it is indeed a good job. That's Be–Think–Say. But the positive approach to language suggests the process can work in reverse; if a man says he has a good job often enough he will come to believe it, and then it is indeed a good job for him. Say–Think–Be.

It follows from this that you can choose to have positive experiences by choosing to use positive language. If you avoid using expressions like 'I can't' or 'it's impossible', you stop putting restrictions on yourself. In arguments, changing 'yes, but' to 'yes, and also . . .' stops you putting restrictions on others.

When you begin to notice the negative or positive value of the language you use, you may be surprised to find that some little words crop up all the time. In our family, one of those was 'should'. That's a word that instantly dampens down a person's power and freedom to choose. We changed it to 'could'. If anyone forgot, we reminded them. It became something of a family joke.

My youngest child was so assiduous about it that she made charts of positive and negative words to remind herself. She even pointed out the negative words to her friends and teachers. I remember on one occasion she told us at tea-time, 'My teacher used the "sh" word in front of the whole class today!' We were all astonished.

'She said "shit"?' exclaimed her brother, scandalized. She gave him a withering look. 'Of course she didn't, silly,' she said. 'Everyone knows the "sh" word is "should"!'

Thinking about the words you use in the family situation can make a surprising difference. Thinking about the words you use in your own inner dialogue can be very fruitful, too.

Take the bullying situation. The Be–Think–Say pattern might go something like this. Your experience has been of a bad situation which has not got better, and which no one has been able to resolve. That's the fact. It leads you to think that the problem won't get better, and no one will be able to resolve it. Then your self-talk may be along these lines – 'She's never going to cope', 'I can't help her', 'The school should do something about it . . .'

The positive approach is to change your self-talk. Then the way you perceive the situation will be affected, and that will affect the situation itself. What if, when you think about the bullying problem, you notice your negative self-talk and opt for positive alternatives? 'She *is* coping', 'I *am* helping her', 'The school *is* doing something about it . . .'

The more you repeat messages of this kind the more you will notice the truth in them. There will be ways in which your child is coping, and ways in which you are helping, and it is possible that the school is doing something about it.

Such a pattern of thinking is less alarming and more hopeful. It will enable you to stop adding your own burden of helplessness and anxiety to your child's, and that will make her situation less overwhelming. She *will* cope better, you *will* be helping . . . Say–Think–Be.

Positive self-talk can take the form of affirmations. This is how affirmations are supposed to work. You decide what you want, and affirm that you've already got it. You use the present tense, and support it with expressions like 'right now' and 'at this moment'. Your conscious mind may balk at the obvious discrepancy between what you are saying and what the actual situation is so it may feel strange and silly at first. But your unconscious mind simply accepts the message in the words.

So if, for example, you feel you are a hopeless parent for not being able to help your child, you don't say, 'I wish I were a great parent' or 'I hope I can become a better parent'. You simply affirm –

RIGHT NOW, I AM A WONDERFUL, SUPPORTIVE PARENT!

You keep on saying it until you start to believe it. Then your anxiety and inhibitions begin to dissolve, and you are able to release the wonderful parent in yourself. For, whatever the enterprise, fear of failure and lack of confidence are bound to compromise your performance and prevent you reaching your potential.

When you use affirmations, avoid negative words altogether. 'It's a great day today', for example, has a much more punchy feel than 'Today is not too bad'.

I have seen claims that even affirmations like 'I am now fabulously wealthy' can come true! I suppose they *can*, in the sense that they become *possible*. You have to be able to conceive of something before you can hope to achieve it.

You can have a lot of fun with affirmations. You can also use them to get you through your darkest hours. Your children might be able to use them, too. Share them, talk about them. Even your bullied child might find she can believe '*At this moment*, I am strong and beautiful and brave!'

■ POSITIVE THOUGHTS

In Daniel Goleman's book, *Emotional Intelligence* (Bloomsbury, 1996), he talks about a 'modern epidemic of depression among young people'. He ascribes this to pessimistic habits of thought that make children respond to relatively minor problems like an argument with their parents or a bad grade by becoming depressed.

Worrying about all the bad things in life can easily make us lose our sense of proportion, and stop noticing the good things.

There's a game that shows exactly how this works, and you might like to try it with your child next time she's feeling that everything's terrible.

Ask your child to look carefully around the room and notice anything that's red. Give her plenty of time. Then get her to close her eyes and tell you everything she can remember seeing that was blue.

She will probably say, 'I can't do it! You told me to look for red! What was the point in that?'

The point is that if you're only looking at red you don't notice blue, and if you're only looking at what's bad you don't notice what's good. The more you decide to focus on the good things in life the more the bad things fade into the background.

Focusing on the good is as easy as ABC.

▨ A Expect the best!

A lot of people expect the worst in every situation because they are trying to protect themselves from being disappointed. This obviously doesn't work because even someone who expects the worst will still be disappointed when things go wrong. Sometimes they might try to protect their children, too, by warning them that they should be prepared for trouble and setbacks, instead of encouraging them to assume that everything will be fine.

If you always expect the best you can live in a state of pleasurable anticipation, whereas if you expect the worst your life is overshadowed by anxiety and dread.

Consider this story:

Jane

Jane is on a camping weekend with her family, and on the very first evening she notices that she's lost the ring her grandmother gave her. Her husband and children search high and low, but there's no sign of the ring.

Her husband takes the view that the ring will show up if it's meant to, and if it's lost then there's nothing that anyone can do about it anyway.

Jane is distraught. She's angry with her husband for making light of her loss, and spends the weekend fretting over it.

Which one would you rather be, Jane or her husband? Which one would you rather live with?

This isn't my story, but it's a true story, so I can tell you what happened in the end. When they took the tent down Jane found her ring on the flattened grass underneath the groundsheet.

So when your child leaves the house in the morning full of anticipation and dread, don't pay into it. Expect her to cope well and enjoy herself. That way you will not only be freeing yourself to get on with the business of the day without worrying about her all the time, you will also be freeing her from the additional burden of responsibility for upsetting you. As well as that, you will be modelling a much more robust approach to life which will inevitably begin to rub off on her.

If you always anticipate the best, you're twice a winner. You not only enjoy a much better quality of life, not worrying about what the future might bring, you will also have a positive effect on what the future does bring.

A friend of mine, for instance, hates her birthdays. She always expects them to be miserable, and they always are. Another friend loves hers. She expects to enjoy them, and she does.

B Trust the process!

Expecting the worst is one way we try to protect ourselves against future catastrophe; the illusion of control is another. We think that if we can just get the right information and take the right action, we can control what happens to us. We can avoid heart disease by cutting down on cholesterol; we can avoid unemployment by working hard and achieving well.

It's an illusion. We may avoid heart disease only to get cancer instead, from eating too much hydrogenated vegetable oil; we might work hard only to find we've become too experienced and too expensive to be employable.

Trying to manipulate the future is not only a waste of time, it's also very tiring. It uses up energy that could be employed better in enjoying the present. It can be a wonderful release just to let it go.

Accepting what happens when it happens is a much less frustrating and anxious way of living. It's an attitude that can grow from the most trivial incidents to have a profound effect on your whole experience of life.

I remember a few years ago, going down to South Cornwall for the day. The weather was glorious, and we walked for miles along the coastal footpath. When we got back to the car we were all really hungry so we drove into Marazion to look for a café. We found the perfect place, but just as we were about to go in the 'Closed' sign went up.

It was half past four in the afternoon. We could have felt annoyed, frustrated, despondent, but we decided to trust the process. We had just set off for home when we noticed a take-away pizza place overlooking the bay. We sat out eating pizzas on the beach. It wasn't what we had planned – it was actually better.

Trusting the process means giving up the illusion of control and accepting that there will be setbacks as well as successes. It means acknowledging that as we can't tell what the future will bring we can't judge our present experience as 'good' or 'bad'. What looks like a problem today – say, you didn't get the job you wanted – could turn out tomorrow to have been a blessing when you get an even better one.

Trusting the process means noticing that every cloud has a silver lining.

▮ C Look for the silver lining

When things go wrong, however big or small, you can choose how you want to react. You can throw up your hands in helpless horror, pack your bags, kick the cat or hit the whisky – or you can, if you prefer, look for what good can come out of it.

If your response to life is generally passive, you may see problems and setbacks as insurmountable, or expect someone else to sort them out. But you can choose to adopt a more active attitude and say, 'What do I need to learn in order to get through this?'

In this way, you make problems into opportunities for growth. Little problems are opportunities for a little growth, and big ones are opportunities for major growth.

Being bullied is a very big problem for a lot of children. Instead of looking on it as an unmitigated disaster, ask yourself, 'What does my child need to learn in order to get through this?' You will see that the skills she needs to develop will make a major difference to her competence and confidence in every area of her life, and for the rest of her life.

The ABC of positive thoughts – expecting the best, accepting what comes and looking for the silver lining – might seem unfamiliar at first. It goes against the grain in a society where people so often feel anxious and despairing, have lost all faith in Fate or God and always try to find someone to blame when things go wrong.

But when you let go of negative thinking life's so much more pleasant that nothing could make you go back to it!

▮ POSITIVE FEELINGS

Focusing on the good things in life will lead naturally to a big boost in one of the most beneficial of positive feelings – gratitude.

I think it's a good idea to set aside a few minutes each day, perhaps before you get up in the morning, to think about all the things you like about your life, and feel grateful. It's a good antidote to the pressure we're under to have what we want instead of wanting what we have.

The positive effects of gratitude are not only emotional. Gratitude has been shown to have surprising and measurable effects upon the body as well. Dr Paul Brand, in his book, *Pain: The Gift Nobody Wants – A Surgeon's Journey of Discovery* (Marshall Pickering, 1993), describes how, after a lifetime working on understanding pain, he came to prescribe gratitude as the most powerful painkiller and the best protection against disease.

The well-established benefits of positive feelings to health also extend to physical performance. Various experiments in kinaesthesiology have shown that muscle power is also affected by how you feel. Bad feelings actually make you weaker; good feelings make you strong. If you want to build up your child's physical stature and presence and help her to have more assertive body language, an injection of positive feelings will be every bit as effective as those self-defence lessons that most bullying books recommend, and most bullied children shrink from in horror.

The most powerful positive feeling of all is love. The more you love the better you feel and, like words and thoughts, you can choose which feelings you use. The least complex way of testing the power of love is in relation to objects, and you can have some fun experimenting with this.

Take any object that has no emotional significance to you. It might be a table, for example. Look at it for a while. Think: I love you, table! Notice how you feel, and any physical response. Now tell that table out loud, 'I love you, table!'

What you feel is your own love energy reflected back. It seems ridiculous, but loving even a table can make your skin tingle and bring a smile to your face. If you try it on something more sophisticated, like your computer or your car, you might be surprised by the result.

The car we drive goes like a dream in the dry weather, but it doesn't like the damp. Until a few years ago, we were resigned to the fact that there would be several damp autumnal mornings every year when we'd just have to get a taxi to take the children to school.

Then, one dismal October day, when the car wouldn't start, one of the children suggested we try a bit of positive love energy. I thought it was rather a long shot, but I got back in and we all began to love the car! Instead of frustration and fury, we gave gratitude for all the times it did start and get us to school; instead of slams and kicks we gave a calming touch.

The immediate effect on all of us was brilliant. The tension and anxiety evaporated, and we were able to accept the situation and feel OK about it. The effect on the car was astonishing! It started first time. Ever since we decided to adopt a loving attitude towards the car, we haven't had to get a taxi once.

My daughter overcame her fear of certain no-go areas in her school by telling them, as she passed through. 'I love you, corridors!' Doubtless her body language became more assertive and self-assured, so as well as experiencing the corridors as less threatening she probably reduced any actual threat to herself. Feeling nervous and uneasy is the best way to attract the attention of people who are looking for someone to intimidate.

Practising positive love on things, where you don't need to worry about what sort of reaction you might get, is excellent preparation for practising it on people. The table hasn't done anything to deserve your love, and it won't do anything to return it; the joy of loving is your gift, which is simply reflected back to you in good feelings. You can choose to love people in the same unconditional way, purely for the joy of loving.

POSITIVE LIFESTYLE

The lifestyle choices you make as a parent will affect your children, too, so if you have a child under stress it's doubly important that you choose things that are likely to promote feelings of well-being and optimism rather than apathy and despondency.

What you watch on television, for example, can have a marked effect on your mood and outlook. Too many programmes about hideous diseases, vicious wars, political corruption and violent crime – and, of course, news bulletins – will not help anyone to develop a balanced and optimistic outlook.

Comedies, natural history programmes, adventure stories and dramas, on the other hand, can make you feel happy, relaxed or pleasantly excited.

A counsellor friend of mine recommends to all her clients a daily dose of something they find funny on television. Watching half an hour of comedy with your family – anything that makes you all smile – will lift your spirits and bring you together. A good laugh has the added benefit of giving a boost to the immune system so it'll be helping to keep your family healthy, too.

You might like to try moving away from violent and depressing television programmes altogether for a week or two. It could feel odd at first, and even perhaps trivial, given the inflated value we place on so-called 'information'. But it's only when you stop watching these programmes that you notice how much gloom and anxiety they generate, and they quickly lose their appeal.

Television itself becomes less of an addiction and more of a choice when you use it in this more selective way, and you might want to spend more of your leisure time doing something else.

Physical exercise is known to reduce mental and emotional stress, which makes it a particularly good option for you and your bullied child. Unfortunately, it is easy to take a lot of the enjoyment, and therefore a lot of the benefit, out of exercise by complicating it with science. When exercise is evaluated in terms of suppleness, strength and endurance, targets set and timetables devised, the whole thing can become more of a task than a pleasure.

If you like to work up a sweat on the squash court then that's the best exercise for you, but it won't be the best exercise for someone who prefers the calm concentration of yoga. Don't think of it in terms of how many calories you burn, or how much fat you convert into muscle – think of it in terms of how keen you are to do it.

For a lot of people a walk around the neighbourhood or a bit of gardening can be hard to beat. You can do these things any time you like, alone or in company, and they have the added advantage of being out of doors, which ecopsychologists believe to be particularly beneficial. The whole point is – enjoy!

As you re-evaluate all your lifestyle choices to see if they are generally positive and upbeat, enjoyment is the key issue. Does the food you eat make you feel good? Do the colours you surround yourself with make you feel cheerful and strong? Do you have enough music in your life? Enough silence? And what about the wonderful power of perfume to evoke moods of calmness or exhilaration?

All this positive action on the home front can bring you to a celebrational style of living that nurtures your own inner strength. It can also help you to recover or develop a style of parenting that will provide the optimum growing conditions for your child's confidence and self-esteem.

Chapter Five

Building Self-Esteem

People who are persistently bullied are likely to suffer from low self-esteem, and people with low self-esteem are likely to be bullied. It's a vicious circle. The fact is that you can't defend yourself effectively if you don't think that you are worth defending.

I think this is the single most painful thing for parents of children who are being bullied – to see their child become more and more self-conscious and self-rejecting. It's also the most puzzling, for how can a child who is so loved and lovable fail to love himself?

The usual advice to parents is to tell your child as often as possible that he's wonderful and that you love him. This certainly won't do any harm but, according to experts, bullied children often have unusually close and loving family relationships anyway, especially victimized boys with their mothers, so telling your child you love him certainly can't be the whole answer.

In this, as in all other areas, your child will learn from what you are, rather than what you say. He won't learn to like himself because you like him; he'll learn to like himself because you like yourself.

For this reason, it's important that you take no notice of any advice that makes you feel bad about yourself, and quite a lot of the conventional tips might well do just that.

Parents are often advised to get their bullied child to join a club, for example, perhaps going along with him the first couple of times. If you aren't a clubbable sort of person, this is not good advice for you, and if your child isn't either, it's not good for him. So just ignore it.

The whole point about self-esteem is that it means accepting yourself *as you are*, and that's what makes generalizations like 'join a club' impractical and counterproductive.

You can help everyone in your family to achieve a high level of self-acceptance by encouraging each member to develop a strong sense of himself as separate from everyone else, and by making your home a place where it's safe to express yourself freely and honestly without fear of rejection.

A STRONG SENSE OF SELF

People who lack a strong sense of self are forced to depend on other people to tell them what they think and feel, and how they should act. This makes them vulnerable, and they tend to need lots of reassurance. They may dislike change, and try to control their environment to protect themselves from un-expected developments.

To develop a strong sense of self, your child needs to experience himself as separate from other people and equal to other people. Good boundaries will help him to feel separate; equal rights will help him to feel equal.

Good boundaries

Making good boundaries is really important and really easy. Some basic points are:

1 Allow privacy

Ideally, everybody should have somewhere they can go to be alone. If your child has his own room, allow him to lock it, or to put up a 'Do Not Disturb' notice that will be honoured. If he doesn't have his own room it will be doubly important to respect his need to be alone sometimes if he requests it.

All children who are old enough to unlock the bathroom door are old enough to lock it, and after the age of about seven or eight most children will not need help with bathing and hair-washing.

As well as physical privacy, we all need the privacy of our own thoughts. Heart-to-hearts are fine so long as no one feels pressurized to say more than they want to, and it should be taken for granted that nobody will listen in to telephone conversations, open letters or read diaries belonging to somebody else.

Finally, it's a good idea for everybody in the family to have a private life, separate from other family members – places you go, people you know, things you do that your partner and children don't join in with. Your child cannot grow up until he develops separate areas of experience that he can gradually move into on his own, and seeing that you have these will help him to develop them, too.

2 Maintain a generation gap

Your child needs you to be in control as a grown-up so that he can see how to take control himself. He needs firm guidelines. It doesn't matter if your child agrees with your standards or not; seeing that you have standards and that you are able to maintain them will enable him to set his own standards as he grows up.

3 Encourage differences

Your child needs to have his own views, develop his own tastes and make his own choices. Don't discourage this by criticizing his clothes, music, friends and so on, but, on the other hand, don't stifle it by taking over. As soon as you share his interest, it isn't *his* interest any more. If you are friends with his friends, they aren't *his* friends any more.

It's great to have some common interests, but if you identify too strongly with your child it will be much harder for him to get a strong sense of himself.

4 *Let everyone be responsible for themselves*

If your two-year-old puts your auntie's pet poodle down the toilet when she's having tea with you, you might feel it's your responsibility. But as your children grow, they need to take responsibility for themselves. As far as possible, let them make their own decisions and take the consequences.

What if your child has a pet, and he isn't remembering to check that it's got enough food and water every day? You might feel, on humanitarian grounds, that you should do it for him. But if he's old enough to have a pet, he's old enough to look after it. Make sure he knows the consequences to his pet of being neglected in terms of suffering and ill-health, and warn him that if he doesn't look after it properly the consequence to him will be that he'll have to give it away to someone else who will. Whatever you do, don't let yourself be drawn into looking after it for him.

Letting your child take responsibility can sometimes be unnerving. When my youngest child was six I found her trying to peel and slice a raw carrot with a sharp knife to put in her packed lunch. I told her off and took the knife. She took it back.

'A positive parent doesn't do anything for a child that the child can do for herself,' she told me, quoting word for word what I had said when refusing to tie her shoe-laces for her the previous day. I showed her how to use a peeler, and forced myself to stand back and let her get on with it.

You can always offer advice and support, but don't take more responsibility than you have to, depending on the age of the child.

In the same way, don't make other people responsible for your choices, either the really major ones like the classic 'staying together for the sake of the children' or everyday things like not going out 'because I knew you wouldn't want me to'.

Equal rights

People who put the rights and needs of others before their own rights and needs are called passive, and passive people can become victims. Aggressive people, who put their own rights and needs first, can become bullies. Assertive people respect other people's rights as equal to their own. Another word for self-esteem is self-respect.

Children can become passive if they are forced to give up their rights, and this can happen in many subtle ways besides through the more obvious means of verbal or physical oppression.

Sometimes a particularly close and happy family can function well as a group because each individual within it has given up the right to express dissent or dissatisfaction. Sometimes a family which is not harmonious will present itself as a happy family because each member has given up the right to tell it like it is.

Children can easily feel obliged to give up their rights if their parents are ill, unhappy or overworked, or if their siblings are very young, very numerous or very demanding. Anything, in fact, that makes a child feel insecure in his parents' ability to love and care for him will damage his ability to speak up for himself. That's why all children are more vulnerable to bullying at times of family stress.

Here are the two basic rights your child needs –

1 *The right to be treated with respect*

No child should be physically, mentally or emotionally abused or humiliated. Sarcasm and swearing are examples of showing disrespect. Try not to talk to your child in ways you would not want him to talk to you.

2 *The right to be heard – but not the right to be right*

Every child should have his opinions taken seriously and his feelings validated without fear of being judged, belittled or ignored. But this does not mean he should necessarily have what he wants.

Respecting the rights of your child does not mean giving up your own power. Your child actually needs to feel confident that you are in control if he is to be able to express his own views and feelings without having to be afraid of the consequences.

A family environment based on good boundaries and equal rights will help children to get a strong sense of themselves as separate and equal individuals; a family environment that provides plenty of opportunities for self-expression will enable them to understand and appreciate what sort of individuals they are.

▪ SELF-EXPRESSION

Emotion and imagination are the foundations of self because they are unique to the individual; they cannot be shared or acquired like practical skills and intellectual knowledge.

▪ Expressing emotions

Acknowledging your child's emotions and your own is important if the child is to learn to trust his emotions, and therefore to trust himself. If you deny your own feelings, what the child senses will be at odds with what he is told and he will become mystified and confused. If you deny his feelings, you are encouraging him to deny them too, and any loss of authentic emotion is always a loss of self.

It can be tempting, especially when someone is trying to express painful feelings, to try to threaten, bribe or cajole him out of them, and almost all of us use humour and irony at times to protect ourselves from painful emotions.

If you talk about your feelings openly and without embarrassment, you will be showing your child that it's safe for him to do so as well. You will also be giving him a language for expressing the full range of his own emotions.

This isn't to say, of course, that you should turn your domestic life into some sort of melodrama. It isn't a question of having more emotion, but of expressing more emotion. So, if you've just had a visit from a favourite neighbour, instead of saying, 'That was nice', you might say, 'I really love it when he calls in' or 'I do enjoy his company'.

If someone's said something horrible to you, instead of just crashing plates in the kitchen and refusing to talk about it, you could say that you're feeling upset, hurt, angry, alarmed . . . Putting into words exactly how you feel is the best way for you to work through your feelings, and it makes other people feel safer because they know what's going on and can respond appropriately.

Besides setting an example in this way, you can encourage your child to express his emotions by simply reading his body language and hazarding a guess. If he's lazing around on the settee, instead of saying, 'Haven't you got anything to do?' you could ask him, 'Are you feeling bored?' Or fed up, lonely, ill, unsociable . . . if that's the way he looks.

Quite often, bullied children do manage to tell someone what's happening, but can't bring themselves to talk about how they feel. This leaves them trying to cope with some very intense emotions on their own. Helping your child to talk about his less difficult feelings will make it much easier for him to share his most frightening ones. Young children who find it difficult to talk about their feelings will often express them in play. You can use a favourite doll or cuddly toy as your mouthpiece – 'Big Bear's worried about you today. He thinks you look sad' – and let your child talk to you through him. Or you can use the toy as a mouthpiece for your child – 'Is Big Bear sad today? What's upset you, Big Bear?'

If your child is too old to talk to his toys, he might prefer to talk to an animal. Children of all ages and, indeed, many adults find they can talk to their pets about their most profound feelings. Even looking after a small animal like a rat or a hamster can teach your child a lot about himself, as well as giving him the experience of being responsible and nurturing.

Expressing imagination

As well as acknowledging your child's emotions, you can help him to express himself creatively. Give him as much opportunity as you can to pursue his interests, even if they don't seem to be helping him to socialize more or make new friends, which are often the things we think that victimized children need. Music, sports, art, cooking, gardening – anything that appeals to him will help him to express and realize his secret dreams and fantasies about himself.

Besides developing his creative skills generally, your child can use creative techniques for dealing with the problem of bullying. You might like to try them, too. Writing and drawing are powerful ways of overcoming trauma because as soon as you create something you become active – you stop being passive and helpless and start to take control.

Writing

Writing is a good way of objectifying experience. When you put your feelings down on the page, you are separating yourself from them. That's why so many people come to terms with extreme suffering by writing a book about it.

But although we in the West are obsessed with the idea that for something to be worth doing there has to be fame or money in it, the act of putting your thoughts down on paper is what matters, and not what happens to them afterwards.

The other Western obsession with having to measure and standardize is also irrelevant here: the value of your writing doesn't depend on whether it's 'good' compared with other people's, but on the fact that it's yours.

In valuing and cherishing your writing you are valuing and

cherishing yourself. Take time to think about it, even if it turns out that a sentence or two is all you need to say.

The least challenging way to begin is with a diary. I prefer to use an ordinary notebook so that I'm not restricted on days when I've got a lot to say, and I don't feel obliged to write anything at all on days when I don't feel like it. A diary can feel like a correspondence with a trusted friend and, just like a correspondence, there will be times when you want to write often and times when you just let things lapse for a while.

Writing letters to all the people involved in the bullying situation can also be good – it's a way of saying everything you're dying to say but can't. For it certainly wouldn't be a good idea to post them!

Even story-writing, if you enjoy that, can be useful because whatever you dream up is coming from your own unconscious mind so your stories will be symbolic re-enactments of your current preoccupations and concerns. Although you may not be aware of any link at all between your story and your life, it will be there, and you will be working out your problems in the lives of your heroes and villains.

Drawing

Drawing, just like writing, is something most of us don't do unless we either feel we're good at it or are getting paid for it, or preferably both. That seems a shame because every child has the urge, the ability and the confidence to create visual images, and in other cultures this is nurtured and valued into adult life.

I like to use self-drawing as a sort of visual diary. You and your child might enjoy this, too. Start off by drawing with your non-dominant hand if you feel inhibited.

Just let your brain idle, as if you are doing a doodle, and then draw a picture of yourself. If doesn't have to be literally like you – for instance, you might sketch in clothes you don't actually possess, or give yourself a different hairstyle. This is a picture of how you feel, not how you look.

Now draw in some background detail. Are you indoors or outdoors? With other people or alone? What plants or animals can you see? What's the weather like?

This exercise calls on the right side of the brain, the non-logical, non-verbal side. It draws directly on your feelings, allowing you to *see* how you feel. Drawing without judging doesn't engage your rational mind at all so it becomes a sort of meditation. That makes it a useful tool for anybody who feels stressed.

If you use paints or pens, choose colours in the same way, not according to how things actually look but in order to express how you feel. Colours have been shown to affect people's states of mind, and even their physical health. Working with pink, for example, can be very soothing, and yellow can be invigorating. Combinations of colours will also produce specific effects – red with orange will feel quite different from red with black.

Any pictures you make, whether they include self-drawing or not, will be expressive of your current state of mind. Making lightning flashes or daggers or raging lions from your anger is a way of transforming it. Making a beautiful garden is a way of finding a place of safety. As you start to work in this way you will probably find certain images recur time and again in all sorts of contexts, and these symbols can become powerful emblems of the self.

You can combine drawing with words by using words as the focus for a picture. One of my children made a beautiful papier mâché frame around the 'Serenity Prayer'. . .

Grant me the serenity to accept the things I cannot change, the courage to change the things I can and the wisdom to know the difference.

Another made a picture of a sunny meadow, with the words.

POSITIVE MENTAL ATTITUDE!

under a huge rainbow.

Spending time on this kind of work is a way of gaining a deeper understanding of the ideas you're trying to develop. It's also fun. It requires very little in the way of materials and no particular skill.

Having the kind of household which encourages creative self-expression doesn't mean that everyone in it is drawing and writing all the time. It's more a question of attitude. 'I'm no good at it' and 'What's the point?' are kiss-of-death attitudes when it comes to creativity. 'Everyone can do it' and 'It's a great way of understanding yourself and the world' mean you are not closing off that avenue for your child.

Giving your child permission to express himself freely means being prepared for the best and the worst. Accepting the best is easy, but self-esteem is about total self-acceptance, and if you are able to acknowledge and accept the dark side of your own nature and your child's you will be showing him that it's possible to accept the dark side of himself.

SELF-ACCEPTANCE

To find out what kind of role model you are in the area of self-acceptance, try this simple exercise.

Stand in front of a full-length mirror and take a good long look at yourself. Turn around to see your body from different angles. Look closely at your face. Examine your hair, your skin, your mouth, nose, forehead. Look into your own eyes. What sort of person do you think you are?

Notice the things you say to yourself inside your head. Now tell yourself out loud, 'Right now, I look wonderful and I love myself just as I am.'

If you found it difficult to look at yourself so closely, or if you were surprised how critical you felt, or if 'I love myself' was hard to say, don't worry. You're perfectly normal. Low self-esteem is a feature of our times.

The problem is that there are all sorts of pressures on us to want only good things – good health, good looks, good jobs and so on. We want to be good parents and have good marriages. When we can't achieve these goals we feel helpless and inadequate. We think there's something wrong with us.

But the only thing that's wrong with us is that we're chasing unrealistic goals. Nobody's perfect. The best we are ever going to achieve in terms of health, looks and the rest is good-and-bad. The only goal we can realistically set ourselves is to accept what we are given and do the best we can with it. This approach is not only nurturing for our self-esteem, it will also enable us to reach our potential much more fully.

Take looks, for example. How many women do you know who are perfectly happy with their appearance? Almost everyone I know has some sort of beauty worry. People who feel fat hide themselves under lots of layers or squeeze into tight undergarments, which make them look self-conscious and uncomfortable. People who feel that they have poor skin, crooked teeth, a big nose or bags under their eyes will limit their facial expressions and look away when they're talking to you. In so many subtle ways we actually draw attention to our imperfections by trying to disguise them, and so we make ourselves less attractive. A woman who is happy in her own skin will look good even if she doesn't conform in any way to our conventional notions of beauty.

In the family context, wanting to be a good parent is going to give you a lot of anxiety and put pressure on your child, and this will show in your relationship. Wanting to be a good-and-bad parent means you're definitely going to succeed. No one has to worry about it. Wanting to have a good-and-bad child means you'll never be disappointed. Wanting to have a good-and-bad marriage means you're much more likely to stay out of the divorce courts.

So, instead of trying to be good, try to be yourself. Your whole self, warts and all. Because, when it comes to being yourself, you're the expert. Do the mirror exercise again. Tell yourself all the things you usually do – 'My legs are too fat . . . my face is too narrow . . . my mouth turns down at the corners . . . I'm a worrier . . .' Now let go of the need to be perfect. You've got fat legs, a thin face, a grumpy mouth and a tendency to fret . . . So what?

When you stop fighting the bad stuff, you're much more able to notice the good. 'I *have* got rather sensitive eyes . . . straight shoulders . . . an elegant neck . . .'

You can say, 'Right now, I look wonderful' because you do – you look wonderfully yourself. You can say 'I love myself' because you are not laying down conditions, and that's what love is.

'I love myself' is the best possible antidote to low self-esteem. So be kind to yourself. Don't criticize or judge yourself or even make jokes at your own expense. Every time you say, 'What an idiot I am!', 'How silly of me!' or 'What did I go and do that for?' your self-esteem takes a knock.

Take care of your relationship with yourself – it's the only relationship that will definitely last the entire length of your life.

It's also the model on which your child will form his own relationship with himself, and getting that relationship right is even more important than going out and trying to make new friends. It's probably a prerequisite of getting new friends anyway. Helping your child to develop or recover his self-esteem when he's being bullied can be difficult. Making boundaries may work against your natural instinct to protect your child and seem to threaten the stability of the family group. Letting him express his painful feelings will be painful for you as well. Accepting your own faults and mistakes and giving yourself love may bring up a surprising amount of resistance.

But it's worthwhile working at it because good self-esteem is the root of psychological self-defence, and just as your child needs to defend himself from the anger and aggression of those who are bullying him you may need to defend yourself from your child's anger and aggression, at least until he learns to use them in constructive ways.

Chapter Six

Using Anger

Anybody who is being pushed around, teased and taunted, threatened and excluded is bound to feel angry.

The good news is that anger is pure energy. It gives us the power to stand up for our rights, to protect our boundaries and to express our most pressing needs and desires.

We talk of anger in terms of heat – we can have a fiery temper, get hot under the collar, engage in heated discussions. Anger is the spark that ignites a burning ambition, a flaming passion. It is generated every time we are thwarted, and spurs us on to greater effort. For a bullied child, it can be the power that turns the situation around.

The bad news is that, just like fire, anger can be dangerous and destructive if it isn't properly managed, and children who are being bullied can easily be overwhelmed by such intense feelings of anger that their normal coping skills are completely inadequate. They can't express their anger directly to the people they are angry with so it builds up under pressure and becomes simply too hot to handle.

Bullied children may try to get rid of their anger in two ways. Some will dissipate it by becoming unusually aggressive and taking their anger out on other people who are not connected with the bullying at all. Others will damp it down by turning it inward and becoming depressed or self-destructive. Many children will do both.

IF YOUR CHILD BEHAVES AGGRESSIVELY AT HOME

You can react in any of four ways:

1 Get angry too.

This increases the general level of anger in the family. It allows your child to alienate you and so lose her most valuable ally. It makes her anger even more frightening and difficult to control.

2 Get angry and pass it on.

This is called 'kicking the cat'. Your child shouts at you for asking her to tidy her room, and that puts you in a bad mood. You snap at your younger child for some trivial misdemeanour, and that makes her angry, too. So she looks around for someone to take it out on . . . Watch out, cat!

3 Feel resentful, but not say anything.

This puts you in martyr mode. Your energy's all tied up with keeping your anger in, and you've none left over to help your child. Also, everyone knows the situation is volatile and you could be about to blow your top at any minute.

4 Remember the game of hot potatoes . . . and give it back.

The key to giving the hot potato back is not to take things personally. Focus on the fact that the anger and bad feelings are her problem, not yours. As soon as they become your problem you are no longer in a position to help your child.

It may be hard to believe, but outbursts of aggression are usually a plea for help. The aggressive child has an urgent need for recognition and reassurance. Make it clear to her that you are willing to listen sympathetically to what she has to say, but only if she talks to you properly, without swearing or shouting. How successful this is may depend upon how well you can manage not to swear and shout yourself.

One way of avoiding being drawn into an argument is to reply to her demands and accusations with a question. If she says, for example, 'You're always getting at me!', you might ask, 'Do you feel that I'm getting at you?' or 'Am I always getting at you?'. Needless to say, these questions should sound neutral and not accusing.

If your child causes problems at home by picking fights with her brothers and sisters, your best bet for defusing the situation is to offer to hear both sides of the argument one at a time, but only if nobody shouts or interrupts. After that, you can try to get each child to look at things from the other one's point of view, by asking them to express their own feelings and imagine how the other feels. They will both have some responsibility for fighting so they can both apologize for their part in it. You don't have to judge which one is right or wrong. Whoever started it, the fact is it takes two to argue, and either one of them could always simply have left the room.

Some children are naturally more aggressive than others, and some have failed to learn how to cope with anger at an earlier age. An aggressive child might have learned as a toddler that she can get what she wants by throwing a tantrum. As using anger aggressively works for her, she may not have had to discover more constructive ways of coping with it.

Fortunately, it's never too late to learn. So as much as you can, try not to give your child whatever she wants when she becomes aggressive at home – don't even give her the satisfaction of drawing you into an argument. But do give her what she desperately needs, and that is to have her feelings recognized and acknowledged. Offering to listen to her if she talks to you properly will be a big incentive; refusing to listen if she's ranting and raving at you will be a powerful sanction.

■ IF YOUR CHILD BECOMES DEPRESSED AND SELF-DESTRUCTIVE

This, also, is a cry for help. But it can be as hard to see how to help a child who is withdrawn and distant as one who is hostile and full of rage.

Once again, the first thing to do is to remind yourself that it's her problem and not yours. If you become anxious and depressed as well, you won't be able to help your child. If you get frustrated and angry about having her moping around all the time, you will simply be reinforcing her own negative feelings about herself.

A passive child may be introverted and withdrawn by nature, or she may have learned to cope with angry feelings by turning them in on herself at an earlier stage.

She may have been discouraged from expressing anger because her parents were ill, fragile, overworked or perhaps afraid of expressing anger themselves. She may have been pacified, rather than satisfied. She may simply have discovered that there was no point in expressing anger because it never got her the recognition she wanted. Perhaps being depressed proved to be a more effective way of dealing with her situation.

If your child is depressed, she will probably not even be aware of the anger that's at the root of her depression. She may not be experiencing anger at all. As anger is such a powerful part of the experience of being bullied, that means she will have lost touch with a large part of herself.

Helping your child to cope with depression requires the same kind of approach as helping her to deal with aggression. First, don't get swept up in her feelings, but stay centred in your own. Second, don't allow her to treat you disrespectfully or thoughtlessly, even though she is obviously struggling. Anything that diminishes you makes you less able to help her so it's important that you stick up for your own rights.

Third, reflect back what she says to you, by answering with a question or agreeing, because that will give her an opportunity to clarify her feelings and express them more fully.

For example, if your child says, 'I just hate my life' you might say, 'You hate your life?' or 'Yes, it is pretty tough for you at the moment'. The more she can explore her negative feelings the closer she will come to uncovering the underlying anger, so don't be tempted to deny her feelings by saying everything's fine, or it's not as bad as all that. Don't try to make it all better by offering distractions or giving special privileges, which will be sending the message that not coping means you will cope for her. Avoid trying to bully her out of her feelings by saying she should pull herself together, she doesn't know how lucky she is and so on.

However hard it is to live with a despairing child, there's no short-cut back to happiness. She's in a process, and it has to run its course. Don't worry if it seems to be taking a long time – try to be patient.

People think of depression in wholly negative terms, which is a pity. You could just as well view it as a refuge in times of conflict or confusion, a safe space where people can go when the stresses of life are threatening to overwhelm them. A friend of mine used to call it Nature's way of making you stop and give your soul time to catch up.

Your depressed child needs to get in touch with her difficult feelings gradually, in her own time. This is inner work, and she may seem terribly remote. But you can help and support her enormously by just being there for her. Sitting and watching television together sometimes is companionable and very un-demanding. Doing jigsaws can be calming and constructive, and the pictures your child chooses will be of things she finds soothing and reassuring. She may want you to join in or she may prefer to do them on her own.

Drawing and painting and any sort of craft work are also good ways of occupying time. If your child likes reading, make sure she's got a plentiful supply of library books. Try not to feel afraid of your child's unhappiness or you will make her frightened, too. Accept it as a fact of life, and help her to live with it until it passes.

Depressed people can often gain strength from the natural environment. Just feeling the earth beneath your feet, even in your own back garden, can be wonderfully grounding. If your child likes the countryside or parks, take her as often as you can, but don't expect her to be particularly sociable. Let her simply be with her own thoughts in Nature.

I know a child who recently suffered some terrible setbacks and feels deeply depressed. All she wants to do is go up on the moors and walk. Her mother takes her and walks with her as often as she can, and they are coming through.

It goes against a parent's instincts to let a child suffer, but when your child is depressed there sometimes isn't a lot else that you can do. Your depressed child needs lots of love and support, but she also needs space to experience her own feelings and learn how to cope with them herself. She doesn't need you to fight her battles, and that includes the inner battle against her own anger. Her pain is what shows that the anger is still alive, a glow among the embers.

Don't be panicked by your child's depression. Look upon it as her way of coming to terms with difficult feelings at a manageable pace. Don't try to rush her, but let her know that you are there for her when she is ready to start talking about things. Remember that many people who have suffered severe bouts of depression and even complete breakdowns say that they have emerged from the experience with wonderful new insights that have helped them to make really positive changes in their lives.

However, it will be incredibly difficult for you not to become frantic and distraught if your child starts to display self-destructive or suicidal tendencies. Climbing out of upstairs windows, walking in front of cars, taking handfuls of painkillers – these are not unusual cries for help. It may comfort you to bear in mind that they very rarely result in suicide. But, of course, they must still be taken very seriously. Your child must be in desperate need to make such desperate cries for help.

I think it's more important than ever with a suicidal child to talk openly about what is going on. Explain to her the possible consequences of her behaviour – that suicide attempts can often result not in death but in drastic and crippling injuries. That thoughts of suicide can become a lifelong habit, and what starts as a refuge from problems can turn into a trap.

Let her know that you are always there for her if she ever wants to talk about anything that's troubling her. Tell her that if she would prefer to talk to a counsellor, you will arrange it for her. Discuss ways of coping with desperate feelings by letting them run their course, instead of panicking or trying to fight them. Help her to understand that time is the great healer, and that simply finding ways of passing time is one way of letting him do his work.

Last, but not least, be sure to tell her how absolutely terrible it would be for you to lose her. Say you don't want her to kill herself, but you realize there's nothing you can actually do to stop her. In this way, you are allowing your child to be responsible for herself. You are also being pragmatic, for there really isn't anything anyone can do to stop a person from committing suicide once they've made up their mind to it.

This is a frightening realization, but it's a vital one. A parent's first instinct when threatened with the loss of a child is to act – to take any measures, however desperate – to protect and save the child. When the threat comes from the child herself the parent's actions can be very counterproductive. You may find that you feel bewilderingly antagonistic towards your suicidal child, and more inclined to try and force her out of her depression than to give her the support she needs.

Be kind to yourself. Remember you might need someone to talk to as well. It's a volatile and alarming situation, but whether you decide to seek help for yourself and your child or not, if your child feels suicidal she is getting very close to a breakthrough. The anger and hatred turned in upon the self has become so intense as to be murderous. The glow in the embers is about to burst into flame.

When your depressed child does manage to express anger, react positively so that she feels it's OK to be angry. Show her that you are not afraid of her anger, and she won't need to be afraid of it either.

Giving your child permission to be angry, whether she tends to turn it out against other people or in upon herself, depends upon your ability to protect your own boundaries. Helping your child to use her anger effectively will depend upon your ability to use your own.

▪ HOW TO USE ANGER EFFECTIVELY

You will probably have many opportunities to practise using anger effectively if your child is being bullied because however hard you try not to be swept along on her tidal wave of rage or despair you will certainly not succeed all the time. You will also have plenty of anger of your own – towards the people who are bullying her, the teachers who aren't protecting her and so on.

It's obvious that ranting and raving or wringing your hands is not going to help at all, but don't worry if you find yourself doing quite a bit of both. There isn't an easy, painless way of dealing with anger. It takes patience, courage, clarity and great effort to get it right, and most of the time we all veer slightly off-centre towards passive or aggressive patterns of avoidance.

Getting it right is much easier if you can adopt a positive attitude towards anger, and develop a clear strategy for dealing with it.

▪ Adopting a positive attitude

It's easy to feel negative about anger because the negative effects of anger are generally more obvious than the good effects. One reason for this is that the good effects of anger are within the individual and the bad effects spill over onto other people.

When I was at school, for example, I did so badly in the practice paper for my chemistry exam that my teacher told me I had no potential in the subject and I should give it up straight away. I was angry because I had worked hard and done well in class up until then, and regarded my 12 per cent total in the practice paper as no more than a temporary hiccup. If I had kicked a few doors in and picked a fight with someone, or become depressed and withdrawn, these would have been very noticeable ill-effects of anger. But, in the event, I simply refused to drop chemistry, revised well and got an A grade. Nobody else would have realized that this unexpected turn-around was purely because I was so outraged at being told I had no potential.

You can see anger at work all the time in sporting activities. If a football player feels he's the victim of a bad referee's decision, for example, things could go in any of three ways: he might become aggressive and abusive, disrupting the game and risking being sent off; he might throw up his hands in disgust and stop trying, or he might use the extra adrenaline rush of anger to sharpen his concentration and make him more determined than ever to score a goal.

No footballer wants to fall victim to a bad decision, just as outside sport nobody wants to be unfairly treated, provoked or thwarted, but these things happen. Anger is an inevitable fact of life, and the difference between someone who is continually stressed and frustrated and someone who achieves his goals will often be no more than a clear strategy for dealing with it.

Developing a clear strategy

Here is a 4-point plan for dealing with anger:

1 recognize it;
2 express it;
3 release the energy;
4 convert the energy into action.

When it goes right, it's brilliant. For example, with my chemistry exam, I knew I felt angry and I knew why: I told my teacher I was angry and refused to give the subject up; I released the energy by not getting stuck in despondency or blame, and I converted it into action by going for an A.

Most of the time, of course, things are not so straightforward, and there can be problems and resistance at any stage. Sometimes we'll know we're angry, but express it negatively. Sometimes we'll be comfortable about expressing anger but then find it hard to let go of blame. Quite often, we don't even get past the first post of recognizing anger for what it is.

1 Recognizing anger

There are many reasons why we might not give ourselves permission to be angry. This resistance can be internal, from guilt if our anger seems unreasonable, for example, or fear of being swept along by the sheer power of angry feelings. Or it can be more to do with how the person we are angry with might react. You won't want to upset a fragile child, for instance, and you won't want to enrage an aggressive one.

But that doesn't mean that the anger just goes away. Energy is indestructible, and the energy of anger, if it isn't recognized and channelled into useful activities, can produce destructive physical, social and psychological effects.

The physical effects of anger, such as heightened blood pressure, which prepare the body for action, will cause physical problems if the anger is unresolved. In the long term, these might include heart disease, which is associated with an irascible temperament, and cancer, often linked to a passive one. In the short term, physical effects can include tension headaches, palpitations, breathlessness, skin disorders, aches and pains and a whole range of other minor problems. Even being accident-prone can be a side-effect of unresolved anger.

In a social context, anger is a way of asserting the self in relation to other people. In the long term, unrecognized anger can disrupt relationships by making a person argumentative or withdrawn, unpredictable, unreliable, evasive or manipulative. Isolated incidents can cause rows over nothing and breakdowns in communication.

The psychological value of anger as a means of self-expression and self-preservation can also be lost when anger is unrecognized, and problems like depression, anxiety and low self-esteem can result.

Whenever you have a problem it's worth checking if the hidden cause could be anger. If you have a headache, or an accident, or a nasty rash, try asking yourself, 'Why am I angry?' If you feel unhappy in a relationship, or if you feel sad for no obvious reason, ask yourself the same question. Really try to be open to all the possibilities, and you may be surprised at what comes up.

Another way to recognize anger, besides by its effects, is by learning its disguises. Words like 'disappointed', 'frustrated', 'bored', can all be used to describe anger without naming it. Exasperated, concerned, amazed, bewildered . . . the list is endless.

Working in this way might help you to know, rationally, that you are angry. The next thing is to know it by feeling it. Angry feelings are very uncomfortable. They arise when there is conflict within the individual between what she's got and what she wants. As long as this conflict is unresolved, there will be some anxiety and frustration. People on both sides of the bullying situation have a low tolerance of frustration, and one of their problems is that they have to act or react instantly to avoid it. This means that as soon as they start to feel angry they must either get what they want immediately, or else immediately give up.

When you feel yourself getting a surge of anger, hold on. Feel the adrenaline rush and the power. Some books recommend breathing in and out slowly to a count of ten. I prefer the discipline of naming ten items in the room under my breath. These are simple ways of holding the energy so that, instead of becoming instantly aggressive or depressed, you give yourself time to choose how you want to react, and express your anger in more positive ways.

2 *Expressing anger*

The most positive way of expressing anger is simply to say you feel angry. There's no need to worry about whether it's reasonable or not – you're describing a feeling, and feelings are not meant to be rational. When you can't tell the person you're angry with directly, acknowledging your anger to yourself will do.

That's really all there is to it. As soon as you start using anger to force other people to change their behaviour or their opinions you turn a healthy form of self-expression into an ugly act of aggression. Swearing, losing your temper, threatening and shouting are all aggressive ways of expressing anger, as, of course, is physical violence.

Other negative ways of expressing anger can be more oblique. Teasing is usually a veiled form of aggression, even in the context of a loving family. When you tease someone, or are teased, listen to the actual words and not to the laughter. What's the literal meaning of what is being said? Would you say it in a serious voice?

Excessive criticism and shaming are also negative ways of expressing anger, as are coldness and rejection.

So just say, 'I feel angry' and explain why, and then be prepared to let it go.

3 Releasing the energy

You don't have to justify feeling angry. You have a perfect right to your own feelings. What you don't have is the right to be right, or the right to get your own way.

If you feel you have to be right, that means you need someone to blame. In order for you to be right, the person you're angry with has to be wrong. Needing someone to blame puts you in a dependent position, and is a way of giving away your power.

In the same way, if anger is linked with getting your own way you become dependent on the person you are angry with to satisfy this need.

Letting go of the right to be right also means letting go of the obligation to be right, and letting go of the right to have your own way also means letting go of the need.

It's in your own selfish interest to let go of blame and the desire to control because otherwise you can't release the energy that your anger generates and convert it into action.

4 Converting the energy into action

The first impulse for converting the energy into action will be physical. Pillow-thumping is often recommended. A brisk walk or run. A game of squash. A burst of singing. Listening to powerful music, like heavy rock or opera. Writing angry letters and painting angry pictures. All these are great ways of getting rid of aggression without losing the energy.

But physical activity is only the first stage. It gives you time to process your anger, to experience its power and to understand what it is that you need.

Why should you need time to understand your anger? Because, when it comes to angry feelings, things are very rarely the way they seem. You may not be angry for the reason you think, or with the person you think, because when the anger you feel is too hot to handle it often gets deflected onto something or someone less threatening. You may not dare to be angry with your boss, for example, so you'll get really heated up about the political situation instead, or pick an argument with your partner.

Whenever you feel angry, particularly if the anger seems out of proportion, try asking yourself, 'What am I *really* angry about?' and 'Who am I *really* angry with?'

As well as being deflected from its true object in this way, anger can sometimes be used to disguise other uncomfortable feelings. You may not want to feel humiliated at getting lost, for example, so you'll become furious that the map isn't clear enough. Quite often, people get angry as a way of avoiding fear. So ask yourself, 'What am I afraid of?'

Say a man is angry with his wife for getting home really late from a night out with her friends. What fears might his anger conceal? There's quite a choice of answers, isn't there?

If you ask yourself these questions whenever you feel angry, you will get some useful information about the situation you are in. If you notice a pattern – things that always make you angry – you will get some useful information about yourself. Do you get angry if you feel criticized? Are you afraid of being criticized? Why?

Do you get angry if people ignore you? What would make you feel better?

Giving yourself time to understand your anger means you will be able to see what you need. Then you can use the energy of anger to start looking for ways of getting your real needs met.

If your child is being bullied she is bound to feel angry. How she deals with her anger will depend partly on her temperament and partly on her past experience, but most of all it will depend upon how she sees you dealing with your own anger. If you tend to shout a lot she will tend to shout a lot; if you slam doors, she will slam doors; if you get physical, she will get physical.

Nobody can feel, express and use anger in positive ways all the time, but if you are always aware of the positive potential in anger you will be able to adopt a positive attitude towards it.

Anger is the root of power, the power to achieve, to succeed, to face healthy competition, the power to know and express the self. For a bullied child, it can be the power for overcoming fear.

Chapter Seven

Dealing with Fear

Fear is a terrible problem for every child who is being bullied.

By helping your child to have enough confidence in you to tell you what's happening, you will have enabled him to overcome his fear of being exposed and shamed as a victim and his fear of having to cope on his own.

By helping him to develop a more positive mental attitude you will have enabled him to overcome his fear that the bullying situation might take over his whole life.

By helping him to recover his self-esteem you will have enabled him to overcome his fear that there might be something wrong with him.

By helping him to experience and express his anger in constructive ways you will have enabled him to overcome his fear of standing up for himself.

Reducing the general level of fear in your child's life helps in two ways. First, it makes him less of a target for bullying as aggressive people are particularly drawn to fearful people and, second, it means he will be better able to focus on the particular fear of being bullied and deal with it effectively.

The first step in dealing with fear is simply to accept it. If your child is being bullied he's in a frightening situation and he's bound to feel afraid. Don't try to protect him from that feeling. As fear is so infectious, you're bound to feel afraid, too. Don't try to protect yourself.

This may seem blindingly obvious, but it isn't. Fear is such an uncomfortable feeling that most of us will go to great lengths not to feel it. Whenever we can we disguise it, deny it and avoid it.

■ DISGUISING, DENYING AND AVOIDING FEAR

Disguising fear is about calling it something else. For example, supposing someone offers you some free air tickets for a trip abroad and you're afraid of flying. You might tell yourself you're too busy, you haven't got anyone to go with, you don't want to feel beholden.

In the bullying situation your child might disguise his fear of going to school by telling himself he feels ill or he's behind with his work. He might even be able to persuade himself that he's being clever by getting out of going to school because it isn't something you would normally allow him to do.

If he's willing to go to school but you're afraid of letting him go, you might disguise your fear by telling yourself that he doesn't look well and he ought to stay at home. Or you might let him go, but find yourself walking down the road with him, as you just happen to have thought of something that means you are going the same way. You are acting out your fear, but not recognizing it as such.

Denying fear does not involve acting it out – it involves ignoring it altogether. When people deny their fear they become reckless and impulsive. They will accept the free air tickets even though they're terrified of flying, and then have a heart attack on the plane.

In the bullying situation, if your child denies his fear he might not bother to avoid risky places and situations; he might actually provoke the people who are bullying him. If you deny your fear, you might force him to go to school even though he's feeling ill or fragile. You might tell him to hit back, even though it's half the football team that's picking on him.

Avoiding fear is about trying to create situations where you are protected from feeling afraid. Avoiders have a great need to be in control. They 'know their limitations'. They're 'realistic'. They wouldn't accept the free air tickets because flying really isn't their thing.

In the bullying situation, your child might try to avoid feeling fearful by simply staying at home. He might give up his outside interests and watch television instead. He might withdraw from his friendship group altogether in case they turn against him, too. If you're avoiding your fear, you might encourage him to restrict himself like this so that you don't have to worry about him so much.

The problem with disguising, denying and avoiding fear is that it doesn't work. Most of us suffer levels of anxiety which are completely out of proportion to the actual dangers in our environment. Fear of illness, for example, is what drives people to see the doctor far more often than illness itself. It also causes them to make changes to their lifestyles which help to reinforce the anxiety by giving constant small reminders of it. Worrying about crime makes people prisoners in their own home, without any actual crime ever having been committed against them.

For your child, trying not to feel afraid is one of the things that will keep him locked into the bullying relationship. He will have to learn to face up to fear, to tolerate it and understand it, if he wants to be free.

FACING UP TO FEAR

What becomes clear when we stop running away from fear is that it's actually a very useful resource.

When we stop disguising it, it can give us a lot of information about ourselves. It shows us our limitations and therefore our opportunities for growth. Until someone can acknowledge it, he's like an alcoholic hiding his bottles – he has no chance at all of getting help and he can't move on.

When we stop denying fear, it can keep us safe. It can help us to work within our boundaries, even while we are striving to push them back.

When we stop avoiding fear, we can let go of the need to control our environment with routines and rigidity. Decision-making is no longer a problem. We can embrace the future in a spirit of adventure, and savour the unexpected.

Without fear, we have no opportunity to experience ourselves as courageous and powerful. Facing up to fear and coming through it brings a feeling of elation. It's the perfect antidote for boredom and inertia, and it's also the root of success, dynamism and personal growth.

So don't be afraid of fear. Show your child how to face up to fear in a positive way. Don't doubt your own ability to cope, or his. If you find yourself thinking that you can't cope, just tell yourself firmly that you can. If you find yourself thinking that your child can't cope, just tell yourself straight away that he can, too.

Here are some practical techniques you can both use for managing fear.

■ SIX SIMPLE TECHNIQUES FOR MANAGING FEAR

■ 1 Breathing

If you feel afraid – or, for that matter, if you feel any strong emotion that threatens to overwhelm you – notice your breathing. This is a very simple way of shifting your focus away from what's frightening you and back to yourself. It helps you to achieve a degree of detachment.

As an added bonus, as soon as you notice your breathing you will automatically begin to regulate it, and calming your body will help to calm your emotions.

■ 2 Finding keepers

Focusing on breathing is a good way of achieving detachment in moments of crisis, but at other times you can use a symbolic object, or keeper, to detach yourself from your fear. Some adults find this hard, but most children are very comfortable with it.

One of my children had a set of worry dolls, for example – she would confide one of her worries to each of them at night, and put them under her pillow. Then she could go off to sleep knowing that her worries were safe until she was ready to take them back in the morning.

My youngest daughter used a doll's teapot in the same sort of way. Every Friday she had a tables test at school, and every Thursday she couldn't sleep for worrying about it. Eventually, she had the idea of putting her anxiety in the teapot and closing the lid on the nights before tables tests. After that she was able to sleep well, she didn't wake up tired and she started to do much better. In a wonderful way, as she learned to worry less she actually had less to worry about.

3 Focusing on the moment

Using keepers is an imaginative way of detaching from fear. A more rational way is focusing on the moment. Most fears are not about what is happening right now, but what might happen in the future.

If you're lying awake, worrying, you can detach by saying, 'Right now, nothing bad can happen so I'll put my fear on hold until the morning.' You might like to write it down, and then make the symbolic gesture of setting it aside. If you're having trouble concentrating on your work because you're afraid your child might be having a hard time at school, you can say, 'Right now, there's nothing I can do about it so I'll put my fear on hold until I get home.'

4 Powerful objects

Throughout history people have used symbolic objects to give them good luck, courage, protection, calmness and clarity.

Journalists and film-makers reporting from war zones will often use powerful objects to protect them. Actors, sportspeople, climbers – people who have to face up to fear in their everyday life – will use such objects. They may not necessarily be concrete things, like items of clothing or jewellery: they can be ritual activities or magic words, like mantras and affirmations.

Some people feel they work because they help you to focus your own energy. A good-luck charm, for example, simply shows you your own potential for good luck, and so magnifies it.

Others believe that certain objects are actually invested with particular powers that you can draw on. Crystals are a case in point.

No one would question that quartz crystals produce energy – they are widely used to power watches and radios. Whether rose quartz could therefore produce a pink energy that would help you to feel more loved and loving, or amethyst a purple energy that would make you feel more spiritual, can't be proven scientifically in the same way, but you might like to experiment with it for yourself.

Go to a crystals shop and just look around. Pick up any crystals you are attracted to, and see how they feel in your hand. Don't ask or read about particular qualities the different types of crystal are supposed to possess – trust your intuition. After you've made your selection, find out what uses your choice of crystal is recommended for. You may be surprised how accurately your intuition leads you towards the very crystal the books say that you need.

There's a whole ritual side to using crystals that your child might enjoy. When you buy a crystal you start by cleansing it of all negative vibrations. There are lots of different ways of doing this, but I like this one best:

Sit quietly with your eyes closed and the crystal in your hand. Take a few deep breaths. Imagine a flame of white fire emerging from the top of your head. Now draw the flame down to your brow, and then to your mouth.

Blow the flame gently over your crystal three times.

The crystal is ready to be programmed with the purpose you

want it to fulfil. This is simply a matter of voicing your intention. It could be as general as 'Give me courage', or as particular as 'Help me to understand this piece of work'.

Crystals are satisfying objects as well as powerful ones. They can be beautiful to look at and good to hold. They carry the magic and mystery of the earth. Boys can keep a piece of polished crystal in their pockets; girls might prefer to wear one set in a ring or pendant. A larger piece of something restful beside the bed can encourage sleep; a clear crystal on the desk can aid concentration.

It doesn't matter what sort of object you or your child choose to give you courage and calmness, and it doesn't matter why such objects work. The fact is that they do. Using objects in this way comes naturally to everyone – we face our first terrifying challenge of separation from our mothers by using transitional objects like teddies and sucky blankets. It's only in the Western world that believing in the extraordinary symbolic power of objects is dismissed as childish and superstitious.

5 Creative visualization

We use visualization all the time in an involuntary way to understand reality. For instance, if I told you I was writing this in a converted stable at the bottom of my garden, you would automatically create a mental picture of me and my stable and my garden.

Creative visualization is only different because it isn't involuntary. It means making mental pictures deliberately to create the reality you want.

There's nothing difficult about creative visualization. It's easy and enjoyable. You simply sit quietly for a few moments with your eyes closed, and relax. Take three or four slow, deep breaths to ease yourself out of your objective situation and into your inner space. Now choose an image that will trigger the sort of emotion you want to feel. For instance, if you're afraid, you might choose to imagine a lion. Experience the image as fully as you can. Feel the hot African sun; smell the dry air; see the red earth, the orange sun, the yellow grass. Hear the breeze rustling through it, and the birds flapping up.

See the lion, massive and majestic, moving slowly. Be the lion. How does he feel? Feel his feelings. You can experience fear-lessness and power without getting out of your chair, and if you practise visualization like this often you will be able to conjure up those feelings instantly by just thinking of the lion, without having to build the whole picture every time.

How you picture your child will make a great difference to how you feel about him and therefore how he feels about himself. If you picture him as a small, frightened, sensitive person in a hostile environment, you will be full of fear for him and your fear will undermine his confidence in himself. You can elect to change the mental image you have of your child, and see him as the powerful, unique person he is.

This works, incidentally, in more general ways. If you want your child to be more polite, for example, simply make a point of always visualizing him as the polite child he can be. You will feel differently about him, he will feel differently about himself and you will get the change you're looking for.

You might like to try creative visualization in other relation-ships as well. A friend of mine was bullied by her elderly mother. Whenever the old lady started on one of her tirades my friend would picture a pink bubble floating down from the sky, growing larger as it fell, and finally engulfing her mother and contain-ing her. Because pink, for my friend, was symbolic of love, this made it possible for her to separate herself from her mother in a loving way.

When my friend could no longer be provoked, her mother gradually gave up trying to provoke her, and they were able to discuss their differences more calmly and reasonably.

Some people like to visualize a star or a point of light just above their heads, protecting them, bringing them good luck and show-ing the way. A guardian angel could produce the same feelings of safety and power.

■ 6 Pushing back your boundaries

Learn how to face your biggest fears by practising on your smallest ones. Set yourself a task of doing something you're very slightly afraid of doing, and promise yourself a reward when you've accomplished it. This might be something like calling someone who intimidates you, or eating alone in a nice restaurant. As you gain confidence in the easiest things, try something slightly harder. Don't be over-ambitious – the important thing is that you feel the exhilaration of facing up to fear and overcoming it, a process perfectly described in Susan Jeffers's wonderful book, *Feel the Fear and Do It Anyway.*

This exercise will help you to notice how many small things you avoid in life because of fear, and how liberating it is to live less fearfully. If you see fear as a barrier you can't go beyond, your life will always be limited, but if you see it as a challenge, you will be continually pushing back your boundaries, and your potential will be limitless.

Using techniques like these for containing and mastering fear can give us an experience of power in specific circumstances. This can be the first step to uncovering the amazing reservoir of power that exists all the time in every one of us.

■ THE POWER OF LOVE

Because fear is such a dreadful feeling we hate and resent people who make us feel afraid.

Hating people gives them power over us because hatred is corrosive – it eats into our lives. We are diminished by it, just as those we hate are made disproportionately important. Hatred is both a cause and consequence of fear.

But loving people is empowering because when you are the one doing the giving you are the one who is in control. Fear cannot coexist with love, and so loving your enemy is the perfect antidote for fear. The problem is, how can this apparently impossible goal be attained?

Years ago, I read about a man who had been imprisoned by the military junta in Greece and beaten so severely that his whole body looked like raw liver. Not a square inch of skin remained its normal colour.

The man didn't make a full physical recovery, but when he was well enough to talk about his appalling ordeal he said he did not hate the people who had beaten him – he pitied them.

I remember finding this story very hard to believe. How could anybody who had suffered such pain and terror at the hands of others not feel full of hatred and hungry for revenge?

It seems to me now that the answer is this – his injuries were so dreadful that if he had allowed himself to feel the huge hatred they could have inspired he would have been utterly over-whelmed by it and the rest of his life effectively destroyed. Love could be seen, in such extreme circumstances, as a sort of instinct for survival. Through love, and his own inspiring strength of character, the man was able to break free from his tormentors and create a new life for himself.

Most people never have to experience such extremes of fear and helplessness, and most people never learn to protect their lives from being eroded by their own small hatreds through the transforming power of love. It can be difficult to make the effort, and they prefer to accept a degree of fear and resentment as an inevitable part of life.

But if your child is being bullied he may feel intense fear and hatred, which will give him a big incentive to deal with it, and you may have such shockingly murderous feelings towards the people who are hurting and threatening him that you are willing to try quite radical methods, too.

If you have been following some of the ideas in this book you will already have made a start on the incredible work of loving your enemies. You will have stopped judging them, by letting go of blame and guilt; you will have accepted them as they are, by not expecting them to change, but rather being prepared to take responsibility for making changes in yourself, and you will have practised loving for the simple joy of loving, without needing any return.

These things can all help to reduce the power of fear and hatred in your life, but it's forgiveness that will finally set you free.

Forgive ... and forget

A lot of people don't want to forgive because they just don't see why they should. The point about forgiveness is that you don't do it for your enemy's sake – you do it for yourself. So change 'Why should I forgive?' to 'I can forgive; I have that power'.

A lot of people don't want to forget. If they have been hurt, they prefer to keep the pain alive by nursing their resentment because they are afraid of being hurt again and they think that this is a way of protecting themselves. But all they are actually doing is allowing the past to poison the present and the future.

Forgiveness means breaking free of the past, including all the pain and fear, and living in the present moment. The ability to forgive can make a huge difference – the difference, in fact, between happiness and unhappiness – and yet it's a very quick and simple thing to do.

Furthermore, you only have to do it once. It's an act rather than a process. If bad feelings come up again after it's done you just say to yourself, 'I've dealt with that, and it's in the past.'

There are different ways of making an act of forgiveness, but my favourite is this.

1 Remind yourself why you are doing it – that is, to free yourself from painful negative feelings.
2 Write down all the things you need to forgive ...
   You hit my child outside the school gate.
   You broke his pencil box.
   You lied to the teacher and got him into trouble.
3 Read through the list slowly, and really let yourself experience the full force of your hatred.

4 Let it go. It's in the past, and it's keeping you there.
5 Screw up the paper, or tear it up, and throw it in the bin. If you prefer, you could burn it or bury it. However you decide to dispose of it, it's a good idea to express what this symbolic action means in words. You can make up your own formula. This is mine.

> I have decided to forgive you and put what happened in the past, where it belongs.
> I don't expect anything from you, or wish you any harm.
> In letting you be free to get on with your life, I am freeing myself to get on with mine.
> So be it.

It may be a tall order to forgive the children who are bullying your child, and you might like to practise on your family and friends first. Start with small things, like your partner forgetting to pick up the shopping on his way home, or your boss accusing you of something you didn't do. See how it feels to deliberately let go and forgive.

Don't forget that you can also forgive yourself for your own failings. This is a way of boosting self-esteem because it helps you to accept your own weaknesses as well as strengths, and it will mean you feel less fearful of making mistakes in the future.

Forgiveness is a way of breaking your bonds and taking control of the situation. The first time your child is able to forgive his tormentors, even if it's just for one tiny insult or incident, he will understand that forgiveness is a way to power.

If your child is being bullied, he is certainly going to experience fear, and you are probably going to feel afraid, too, on his behalf. The only way you can avoid being over-protective, which could prevent him from dealing with his fear effectively, is by dealing effectively with your own.

Dealing effectively with your fear means first of all acknowledging that you feel afraid, and then using whatever methods you need to help you not to let your fear stop you from getting on with your own life and letting your child get on with his.

If you can also try to live less fearfully in other areas of your life, you will be providing a good role model for your child. You will be helping him to see that even something as apparently negative as fear can carry valuable lessons about courage and love.

Chapter Eight

How Helping Your Child can bring Insights for You

Working through the ideas in this book with your child may lead you to share some surprising insights into your family life and attitudes. It may also bring insights that you can't share with your child – insights that are particularly about you, about the amazing business of being a parent and about the broader social context of your life.

▪ THE HIDDEN HERITAGE

When you discover how much you can help your child to take control of her situation and rise above it simply by being a positive, confident and assertive role model, you are bound to ask yourself sooner or later, 'Could it have been victim attitudes in me that made her vulnerable in the first place?' Worse still, could it have been bullying attitudes? For passiveness and aggression are both sides of the same coin.

Passive behaviour, like aggressive behaviour, arises out of the idea that people are not all entitled to equal rights. In passive and aggressive ways of thinking, there must always be winners and losers. It's very difficult, for example, for passive or aggressive people to simply agree to differ.

Aggressive people take control of the situation because they feel it's their right. Passive people may not feel they have the right to take control, but that doesn't mean to say that they don't want to. They may develop less direct methods of getting their own way – by becoming ill or angry or upset if they don't, or by simply withdrawing their love. This doesn't look like bullying but, if it means that someone else's rights are being overridden, it is.

Generations of women have had to develop such strategies quite deliberately to gain some control in an unequal relationship with men, but passive–aggressive behaviour is often not conscious at all.

The idea that you could have been in any way a bullying parent is a painful one, and you might want to dismiss it out of hand. But unless thinking positively, having high self-esteem and the rest all came very easily to you, any problem areas will already have started to expose aspects of yourself that you were probably quite unaware of before.

For example, until I tried not to say anything critical for a whole hour, I had no idea how judgemental I could be. Until I made up my mind always to expect the best, I had never noticed how much of my thinking was negative and catastrophic.

Passive–aggressive behaviour comes from the experience of being a victim, and victim attitudes can run through families like an underground stream. They may surface in small verbal clues, pet phrases like 'It's not my fault', 'I can't because . . .', 'I never got the breaks', 'Someone ought to do something', 'But what if . . .?'. They may manifest themselves in patterns of addiction or underachievement, but no one notices them because they are just part of the flavour of family life, and have probably been so for generations.

Having a child who is being bullied makes you a victim too. It can reawaken painful victim feelings in you that date back to your own childhood. Experiences of helplessness, rage and terror can be overwhelming in childhood, and children learn to develop coping mechanisms that sidestep or disguise their difficult feelings if they are not helped to resolve them. Childish insecurity, for example, can harden into inflexibility in adult life. In this way, such feelings become invisible.

Having a child who is bullied gives parents a second chance to recognize and resolve victim issues in themselves, this time with adult help – their own. It's a painful business, but the good news is that simply recognizing these unconscious issues is enough. As soon as they become conscious, they stop having a negative influence in your life and are no longer a hidden heritage for your children.

THE MAGIC MIRROR

When you see that your child's victim attitudes could have contributed to her situation, and that those attitudes could have filtered through to her from you, you may begin to wonder if there are other unconscious issues you are passing on to your children without even being aware of it.

The good news is that you can see exactly what these are simply by looking at your child. Children live out their parents' unlived lives, and so they are like magic mirrors, showing us the secret side of ourselves.

Suppose your child has a terrible problem with shyness. You may not be aware of any such problem in yourself because you have learned to adapt to it. You avoid challenging situations, perhaps, or have found ways of disguising your discomfort. But the fact that your child has this problem points to an unresolved issue in you. If you recognize it and address it in yourself, you will not only break free of the limiting adaptive behaviour you've developed over the years, you will also find that it stops being a problem for your child, too.

If you find the idea that children mirror what we can't see in ourselves quite hard to take, it might be easier to see it in other families first. Notice what your friends say about their children.

'Jamie's so stubborn!'

'Andrea's so wilful!'

'If only Simon weren't so shy!'

Jamie's mum might not think of herself as stubborn, or Andrea's as bossy, and Simon's dad might not see himself as shy, but these things could well be glaringly obvious to their friends.

You might say, I haven't got any problems! But actually, everybody has problems; everybody needs problems, or they wouldn't be able to grow. People who think they haven't got any problems are simply projecting them onto someone else.

Supposing, for example, you're afraid of dogs, but you can't face the fear and deal with it. If you project your fear onto your child, and she becomes afraid of dogs, two things happen. First, you feel confident in comparison with your child, and second you can protect yourself from having contact with dogs under the guise of protecting your child.

In a family situation, one sensitive child can carry the whole family's unacknowledged problems. Having a child who is identified as the cause of all the family's anger, anxiety, shame or disappointment means that the real causes don't have to be examined. Children like these are the black sheep in otherwise functional families. They are often called 'difficult', which is the word Alan Train uses in his excellent book to describe both victims and bullies.

Parents of 'difficult' children may have a particular need to find ways of acknowledging their own difficulties and taking responsibility for them. But actually one of the best things parents can do for their child is to find out as much as they possibly can about the dark side of themselves.

▦ SEEING THE SHADOW

A child learns by what her parents are, rather than what they do. The problem is that no one knows exactly what they are, because besides the known, conscious area of the self, there is a whole vast unconscious hinterland.

Imagine that your life is a film. You're producing it, directing it, acting in it and trying to make it just the way you want it to be. All the bits you don't like finish up on the cutting-room floor, and you forget about them. You don't even remember exactly what they are.

But that's not the end of the story because when a child comes along she will inherit not only the conscious, accepted parts of her parents' personalities but all the unconscious parts as well. Her life's film includes all the censored and rejected reels from yours. Sorting through your unwanted stuff uses up your child's energy and resources, and stops her getting on with the creative task of realizing her own potential.

The most empowering thing you can do as a parent is to have another look through all the stuff on the cutting-room floor. By trying to rediscover the parts of yourself that you may have rejected, or uncover the parts of yourself you may never have realized, you will be creating more balance in your own life and leaving less unfinished business for your child to tidy up.

Everybody has the potential to be everything. As John Lennon suggested, we're all Hitler and we're all Jesus. If you see yourself as entirely hard-working and conscientious, you may be overlooking your capacity for laziness and impulsiveness, and these will become an issue for your children. They may become driven, like you, or completely lacking in drive, but unless they manage to achieve the balance in their lives that you have not achieved in yours, they will pass the same either-or choices on to their own children.

You can gain access to the cutting-room floor of your own unconscious in lots of ways without having to go into therapy or dream interpretation. All the information is there in your day-to-day life. It's just a question of learning how to see it.

Carl Jung called the unconscious side of the self the shadow. The fact that it is unconscious means that you can't see it in any direct way – you can only glimpse its reflection. As soon as you understand that what you are seeing is your own shadow, it stops being unconscious and falls under your conscious control. This process is sometimes called withdrawing projections.

Glimpsing your shadow is incredibly easy if you know where to find it, and have the courage to look.

First of all, of course, you can just look at your child. What are her problems? They could be yours. What are her strengths? They could be your unrealized dreams and potential. It isn't only faults and flaws we consign to the unconscious. It can be good things that we perhaps didn't recognize as such, like creativity, for instance, if we grew up in a family system that valued conformity. It can be qualities that children are often told off for – like wilfulness and pride – which can actually underpin success in adult life.

Now look at the people you know. Think of the three people you dislike the most, and write down their names. Taking one at a time, list all the things you dislike about them. When you've done that, think of the three people you like the most, and list all the things you like about them. You have listed your own unacknowledged faults and strengths.

One of the things that I discovered when I did this was that I was unreliable. I couldn't believe I'd never realized it before. I was always promising to go places and do things, only to change my mind at the last minute. If I'd noticed it at all I'd put it down to natural exuberance – I just couldn't say no – or just plain busyness. Being aware of the problem means I don't make so many promises these days, and when I do promise to do something I make a conscious effort to stick to it.

Here are some other ways of getting a glimpse of your shadow:

1 Slips of the tongue

When you say something you didn't mean . . . your shadow did.

Consider what it tells you about yourself, and why you don't want to recognize it.

2 Actions with unwanted consequences

If you do something that accidentally upsets someone, or disrupts something, ask yourself, What is it in me that wants this outcome? Why am I reluctant to admit it?

Ask the same questions also if you inadvertently do something that delights someone or makes something possible.

3 Things people say about you

If someone criticizes you, resist the temptation to react defensively, and treat what they say as a possible piece of useful information. Nobody's perfect.

Similarly, if someone praises you, resist the temptation to dismiss what they say. They could be showing you something great about yourself you haven't managed to acknowledge.

4 Physical ailments

The psychological aspect of physical symptoms is widely accepted these days. Most ailments have obvious verbal connections, which can be worth noticing. We use the word 'headache', for example, as a synonym for 'problem'. If you've got a pain in the neck, what or who is being a nuisance? If you suffer from stomach trouble, what is it that you can't stomach?

Look at the effects of your physical symptoms. Do you get a lot of colds and infections which mean you need to stay away from other people? Perhaps you have a strong unconscious need for more personal space and time to be on your own. If you make that conscious, and take the time you need, you may find that you stop getting all the bugs that are going round.

5 Humour

When you joke about something, look at the actual words you use. What do they mean, joking aside? We know that teasing can be a way of masking aggression, but humour can also mask a whole range of other unacknowledged attitudes. Self-deprecating jokes, for example, may express a person's deepest fears and suspicions about herself.

6 Opposites

Every emotion contains the potential for its opposite. Couples who have been passionate partners in marriage can become bitter enemies in divorce.

Think of all the people and things you feel strongly about, and imagine that you hold the opposite view. What would this tell you about yourself? Why is it something you don't want to know?

Seeing the shadow side of yourself is really just a question of being open to other possibilities besides the way things look. It's about seeing yourself the way you don't want to see yourself, as well as the way you do. It doesn't happen all at once because no one can ever uncover all there is to know about herself. It comes in moments of insight, which can be both liberating and traumatic.

If you want to try opening up to all your possibilities, you will need to approach it in a non-judgemental way, and be ready to give yourself all the love and forgiveness you need.

PARENTING THE INNER CHILD

Another way of uncovering your hidden agendas is called inner child work. The idea here is that we all carry inside ourselves the child that we once were.

Our unresolved childish feelings can be reactivated by events in later life, and this in turn sets up a sort of instant replay of all the things our parents said to us in similar circumstances when we were little.

According to this scheme of things, we each have three inner voices – the inner child, the inner parent and the mature adult.

The inner child will usually express herself in terms of feelings because children are feeling beings, who haven't learned to rationalize and detach themselves from their emotions. The parental voice is usually critical. The inner child might say things like, 'It's not fair', 'Why should I?' and 'You don't like me'. The inner parent will be more on the lines of 'Don't be silly', 'Act your age' and 'Stop whining'.

If your parents were particularly controlling, your inner dialogue might run something like this:

Child – 'I want to go out.'

Parent – 'No, you don't.'/'Well, you can't.'
Child – 'I don't want to go out.'
Parent – 'Yes, you do.'/'Well, you've got to.'
Your behaviour will be self-sabotaging because whenever you want something it triggers the parental veto, and the parent in you will not allow you to have it.

As long as this pattern is unconscious, you have to go on acting it out, and something will always stop you getting what you want. Noticing the parent–child dialogue means you can intervene – in the mature adult voice.

Supposing you want a holiday. Your inner child says, 'I want a holiday!' Your inner parent says you can't. Now bring in your mature adult. Acknowledge the child's feelings, and take them seriously. Then, even if you decide you really can't go this time – because you're low on cash, for example – you are breaking the 'I want–You can't' connection by introducing a third point of view – 'Perhaps it will be possible.'

As your children grow, they will trigger feelings in you that you experienced at the different stages of your own childhood, and your first reaction will be to go automatically into your parent-voice. Noticing when you sound like your parents, and introducing your own mature adult point of view, will be helpful whenever your children challenge you.

This isn't to say that your parents were not good parents; they were certainly doing the best they could with the knowledge they had. But you live in different times, and you can add to that sum of knowledge, just as your children will add to yours. In this way, parents mature and grow through the experience of parenting. It's evolution.

There are many books about inner child work if you want to go into it in depth, but in the meantime here's a simple exercise. Many counsellors use it with clients of every description, although it was originally devised by Penny Parks for victims of abuse in childhood. It comes from her book, *Rescuing the 'Inner Child'* (Souvenir Press, 1990), which contains a detailed description of this kind of self-help work.

1 List half a dozen childhood experiences which you remember as being upsetting or disturbing.
2 Choose one of them.
3 Write a letter from the adult you to your inner child, asking her to describe what happened.
4 Write a letter from your inner child, describing the event. Take enough time to really think yourself back into it. (Have a tissue handy!)
5 Write thanking your inner child for sharing that horrible experience. Sympathize. Give the mature adult point of view. Tell your inner child that you will always be there to offer love and support whenever she needs it.
6 Write a rescue scene. Go with your inner child into the experience and then do whatever you like to protect her and save her. You can be as violent as you like! You can have superhuman strength! You can fly! Make it as epic and dramatic as you want to, and enjoy it.

Looking for the shadow and getting to know your inner child are ways of finding out things you didn't know about yourself, or had forgotten. The better you know yourself the less of your unseen baggage your child will have to carry, and the more she will be able to be her own, authentic self.

This work will not only bring you insights into yourself and your family. It will also uncover things you may not have noticed before about your whole social environment.

▓ A BULLYING ENVIRONMENT

Asking yourself, when things go wrong, 'What does this tell me about myself?' and 'What changes can I make in myself to resolve it?' is the way to turn your problems into opportunities. It's how not to be a victim.

When you start working in this way you may be surprised to notice that taking personal responsibility goes very much against the social grain.

Whenever there's an accident, a disaster or even a simple mistake, everyone looks for someone to blame. Children who fail are taking their schools to court. Sick people are suing their doctors. The man in the street blames the politicians, and the politicians blame each other.

When we aren't blaming other people, we're blaming our situation. We're encouraged to believe that our well-being depends upon external criteria – we need to have the right car, job, house, in order to be happy. Instead of taking responsibility for our own happiness by learning to value what we've got, we blame what we haven't got and stay dissatisfied. As soon as we get one thing, we go on to want another. In this way we make ourselves the helpless victims of circumstance.

Besides always looking for something that will make us happy, we are encouraged to expect instant gratification for all our needs, and this attitude erodes our capacity for tolerating frustration, which is one of the problems bullies and victims share.

And we are so full of fear! We're afraid of illness, unemployment and crime, of commitment and divorce, of parenthood and childlessness, of death. The prevailing attitude is not to face up to fear with a muscular acceptance of the way things are, but to manipulate circumstances so that we can avoid it.

In these and many other ways, the world we live in can make victims of us all. But here's the good news. Social change starts from the individual. When you change your own attitudes you will see an instant knock-on effect in the attitudes of your family and friends. As they, in turn, change, the people around them will be affected too. The butterfly flapping its wings eventually has an effect, even on the far side of the globe.

Conclusion

Your Powerful Child

There is the paradox that when a child is born he is both incredibly helpless and incredibly powerful. He has the power to make people love him unquestioningly and unconditionally, to lay down their lives for him if needs be.

A bullied child needs more than ever the powerful experience of being loved unconditionally. As long as you want him to change – to be less unhappy, less vulnerable, less fearful, more assertive, more outgoing, less angry – you are not accepting him just as he is. But making changes in yourself – making yourself happier, and so on – and mirroring them for your child is an act of unconditional love. It will bring the changes in your child that you are looking for, without carrying any element of rejection.

Love is one thing that gives a child power; the other is knowledge. Your child needs to know:

- that although he can't choose the way people behave towards him, he can choose how he responds
- that although he can't choose what happens in his life, being happy is a positive personal choice
- that he is a unique and wonderful person, with exactly the same rights as everybody else
- that he can use the power of his anger to protect himself, without having to attack anybody else
- that fear is the only way to experience courage, and facing up to fear is the only way to grow.

If your child can learn these lessons, they will not only help him to be less vulnerable and afraid of bullying, which in turn will mean the bullying will stop. They will also help him to be less vulnerable and afraid of everything, and this will enable him to reach his full potential in all the different areas of his life.

Further Reading

(Those marked ☺ are suitable for older children, and highly recommended.)

My top six

Bradshaw, John, *Creating Love*, Piatkus, 1992
☺ Hastings, Julia, *You Can Have What You Want*, Touchstone, 1992
☺ Hay, Louise, *You Can Heal Your Life*, Eden Grove Editions, 1988
☺ Jampolsky, Gerald, *Love is Letting Go of Fear*, Celestial Arts, 1979
☺ Jeffers, Susan, *Feel the Fear and Do It Anyway*, Arrow, 1991
☺ Robinson, Bryan, *Heal Your Self-Esteem*, Health Communications Inc., 1991

Other great books

Bradshaw, John, *Healing the Shame That Binds You*, Piatkus, 1988
—, *Homecoming*, Piatkus, 1990
Covitz, Joel, *Emotional Child-Abuse – The Family Curse*, Sigo Press, 1986
Harris, Thomas, *Staying OK*, Arrow, 1995
— and Bjork, Amy, *I'm OK, You're OK*, Cape, 1985
Hay, Louise, *The Power is Within You*, Eden Grove Editions, 1991
Holbeche, Soozi, *The Power of Gems and Crystals*, Piatkus, 1989
Lawrence, Anne and Denis, *Self-Esteem and Your Child – A Guide to Happy Parenting*, Minerva Press, 1996
Lindenfield, Gael, *Confident Children – A Parent's Guide to Helping Children Feel Good About Themselves*, Thorsons, 1994
Madow, Leon, MD, *Anger – How to Recognise and Cope with it*, Scribners, 1972
Parks, Penny, *Rescuing the 'Inner Child'*, Souvenir Press, 1990
Peck, M Scott, *The Road Less Travelled*, Arrow, 1990
Skynner, Robin, *Family Matters*, Methuen, 1995
Zweig, C. (ed.), *Meeting the Shadow – The Hidden Power of the Dark Side of Human Nature*, Tarcher, Putnam, 1991

On creative self-expression

Edwards, Betty, *Drawing on the Right Side of the Brain – How to Unlock Your Hidden Artistic Talent*, HarperCollins, 1993

Gawain, Shakti, *Creative Visualization*, Bantam, 1982

McNiff, Shaun, *Art as Medicine – Creating a Therapy of the Imagination*, Piatkus, 1992

Storr, Anthony, *The Dynamics of Creation*, Pelican, 1976

On bullying

Lawson, Sarah, *Helping Children Cope with Bullying*, Sheldon Press, 1994

Mains, Barbara and Robinson, George, *Stamp Out Bullying*, Lucky Duck Publishing, 1991

McLeod, Mary and Morris, Sally, *Why Me? Children Talking to ChildLine about Bullying*, ChildLine, 1996

Tattum, Delwyn and Herbert, Graham, *Bullying – A Positive Response. Advice to Parents, Governors and Staff in Schools*, CHIE, 1990

Train, Alan, *The Bullying Problem – How to Deal with Difficult Children*, Souvenir Press, 1995

Useful Addresses

Australia

National Children's Bureau of Australia
PO Box 686
Mulgrave North
Victoria 3170

United Kingdom

The ABC (Anti-Bullying Campaign)
10 Borough High Street
London SE1 9QQ
Tel: 0171 378 1446
Support group for parents whose children are being bullied at school.

British Association of Counselling
1 Regent Place
Rugby CV21 2PJ
Send an A5 SAE for a list of counsellors and counselling organizations in your area.

Childline
Tel: 0800 1111
Telephone counselling. Can often advise you where to go for help.

Education Otherwise
36 Kinross Road
Leamington Spa
Warwickshire CV32 7EF
Tel: 01926 886828
Support for parents educating their children at home.

Samaritans
Local telephone numbers in your local directory. Counselling for older children and adults, mostly by phone, but sometimes face to face if preferred.

Youth Access
Magazine Business Centre
11 Newarke Street
Leicester LW1 5SS
Tel: 01533 558763
Counselling agency which can give you details of youth counselling services available in your area.

United States of America

Committee For Children
2203 Airport Way South, Suite 500
Seattle
WA 98134
For parents and teachers.

I Don't Care Club
Rachel Bradley
420 Strickland Street
Glastonbury
CT 06033
For children.

The National Association for Self-Esteem
1775 Sherman Street
Suite 1515
Denver
CO 80203

National Crime Prevention Council
1700 K Street, NW
Second Floor
Washington, DC 20006–3817
Can help children.

National School Safety Center
4165 Thousand Oaks Blvd, Suite 290
Westlake Village
CA 91362
Association for parents and teachers.

Parenting Press
PO Box 75267
Seattle
WA 98125
Publishes books on common problems, including bullying.

Parents' Resource Connection
5102 Deerwood Lane
Bemidji
MN 56601
Listing of publications and support groups for parents.

Web Sites

Family Planet — http://family.starwave.com
National Crime Prevention Council — http://www.weprevent.org
The Safe Child Home Page — http://safechild.org

Index